Ellen Bystrøm

Printing
on Fabric

Basic Techniques

 Van Nostrand Reinhold Company

New York Cincinnati Chicago Toronto London Melbourne

Original Danish edition copyright © 1967 by Høst and Son, Copenhagen

Library of Congress Catalog Number 76–123381

Printed and bound in Great Britain
by Jarrold & Sons Ltd, Norwich

Published by Van Nostrand Reinhold Company
A Division of the Litton Educational Publishing Inc.
450 West 33rd Street, New York, N.Y. 1001
Published simultaneously in Canada by
Van Nostrand Reinhold Company Ltd

16 15 14 13 12 11 10 9 8 7 6 5 4 3 2 1

The projects in this book are by students and the author.
Drawings and diagrams are by Grete Petersen and others, based on sketches by the author. Photographs are by Inga Aistrop, Jonals Co., and Jens Sørensen

CONTENTS

FOREWORD

In spite of the abundance of inexpensive machine-made articles that our technology makes available to us at every hand we are presently witnessing an amazing renaissance of interest in many of the old time-honored hand craft techniques.

One such technique is hand printing on fabric, a technique that is becoming increasingly popular and that has special appeal for young people as a means of creative self-expression in a world that grows daily more and more mechanized and impersonal.

Our book is intended as an introduction to this craft. It starts with easy beginning projects and proceeds step by step to more advanced work. For those already skilled in the craft, the index will serve as a guide to projects of specific interest. The instructions given are based on many years of working with students; they have been carefully organized to help beginners avoid the typical "first" errors. As in other crafts, there are a number of methods, all good; the author has selected those that are easiest for the beginner and at the same time do not sacrifice the beauty and usefulness of the completed article. After all, technique is a means, not an end in itself; it will be most successful when the method suits the purpose intended.

Most of the designs given here are eminently suitable for beginning projects, for gaining confidence and developing skill. However, it is the author's hope that the users of this book will go on to create their own designs, and for this reason has included helpful hints for original designing. When you design your own prints for your own choice of fabrics, you will find true creative satisfaction in this craft.

Ellen Bystrøm

BACKGROUND

Potato printing, and other vegetable stamps—not just for children

Probably many of us have tried to print with potatoes at one time or another; it is very likely the simplest method of printing that exists. Therefore we begin with the potato print, not only because there is much to be learned from the experience but also because beautiful and amusing results can be obtained.

WHAT IS A PRINTING STAMP?
The answer to this question appears self-evident, but let's answer it anyway. If you cut a pattern into a flat surface and cut away the background, and if this "raised" pattern can then be transferred to

Use patterns that are as simple as possible when you potato-print.

Cut out a potato and ink it with a brush. Print on paper. Notice the carrot with the star pattern on the cutting board. You can also use a potato peeler to cut patterns in potatoes. Make a trial print before doing the real thing.

5

Cut out a mirror image for letters and figures that have a right and left side. This is a stamp for the letter L. When you print a row, turn the stamp for each print and you can make a decorative border with it.

Materials

A raw, unpeeled potato, not too small.

A sharp, pointed pocket knife or other small knife. A bobby pin. A linoleum cutter set.

Opaque watercolors (tempera), available at art supply stores in boxed sets with a varying number of colors. Later you will need tempera for sketching, so buying this now is a good idea.

Watercolor brush (preferably flat), a small piece of foam rubber, and a clothespin.

Paper napkins for cushioning while printing.

Brown paper or newspaper to protect the table.

Absorbent paper, cheap drawing paper, duplicating paper, typewriter paper or untreated wallpaper.

a piece of paper, after it has been inked, you have made a stamp and you can print with it.

The print will appear as a mirror image. This doesn't matter if you are using a rectangle, circle, or triangle, but if you are using a letter, an "L" for example, the foot of the L will point to the left instead of to the right, if you have cut it in the block as we normally see an L. If you want to make an L, or some other figure that has a right and left to it, the L, or the figure, must be cut out in the block in reverse, so that it will be correct when printed.

THE POTATO PRINT

Take a potato and wash it. Cut through it with an even cut across or lengthwise. Rub both halves against a newspaper; place on another piece of newspaper, cutside down to absorb the moisture; set aside to dry for half an hour. Now you can cut out a figure in the surface of the potato. (Place a newspaper under your work.) The figure you cut should be quite simple. Complicated curves and curlicues are not suitable for the potato. Start with a simple geometrical figure such as a triangle or rectangle. Try to cut freehand— initially we are only concerned in learning the technique. Cut out the background of the pattern to a depth of about $\frac{3}{16}$ in. below the part of the potato you want to make up the print.

Now we're ready to print. Place two or three paper napkins underneath the paper you are going to print on. The print will be prettiest if you use a soft cushioning or padding. (Remember to cover the table with brown paper or the like for protection.)

Paint opaque watercolor (tempera) evenly on the raised part of the potato. You can obtain a better print if you dab a piece of foam rubber into the wet watercolor and then daub it on the potato. (Dissolve a little of the tempera in a small pan or egg cup.) You can use a clothespin as a handle for the foam-rubber dauber. Now you are ready to use the potato as a stamp to print.

By doing the following first experiments, you will learn something about printing with a stamp:

● If you stamp several times, one over the other (either half or whole), you will make the imprint thicker and more dominant.

● When you make a border, you can create variety by letting the imprints appear alternately dark and light.

● If you print several rows, one below the other, in the same pattern, the many little imprints will form a large pattern that fills the area.

● If you turn the stamp at different angles as you print, you will

6

develop new patterns. In this way you can make many little prints into different large patterns.

● A figure that is simple may be used to form patterns when it is repeated.

If you cut out a pattern on the other half of the potato, you may combine the stamps for patterns and borders by printing alternately with the two stamps. You can print pictures. In the photograph of the matchboxes on page 9, the middle one with the sun is printed using two stamps. The sun is cut out in one potato and the rays in another one.

You can also print in two colors with a potato stamp by using a different color at every other or every third print. Or you might print one row in one color and the next row in another color. Before you apply a second color on the potato stamp, you must clean the stamp by stamping out the old color on a newspaper.

If you print with two stamps, you can use one for each color.

Whether you print with one or two stamps, you can make an overprint by letting one print cover some part of the other. On the

Cut the potato away close to the pattern so you can place the print accurately. A handle will make printing easier.

Instead of a brush, use a piece of foam rubber in a clothespin to apply the color.

This is an ordinary nylon shopping bag lined with fabric on which we printed a potato pattern.

Make the pattern in the potato by cutting the potato in two with a deeply serrated knife. Use two shades of the textile colors. Some of the prints overlap, but in general they are fairly well lined up underneath each other. This keeps the pattern from becoming too busy.

7

Background   fabric lining of the net shopping bag shown we used two brown colors printed over each other. The same method was used on the front and back matchboxes and on the cigarette holder shown in the photograph on page 9.

HELPFUL HINTS

Instead of cutting out the pattern in a potato with a knife, you can use a bobby pin (kirby grip). Use the bent part to scoop out with.

Instead of using tempera (opaque watercolor), you can print with marking ink. Marking ink makes a durable print on fabric. You can also use a felt marker.

You can use textile colors instead of watercolors. We will discuss these colors later. They are available in hobby shops or you can mix your own.

If you prefer to draw the pattern on the potato before you cut, use a water-soluble-color pencil or ink marker.

You can also draw with black ink on parchment paper—put the paper against the cut surface of the potato and transfer the pattern by pressing the paper against the potato with your finger. However, too much sketching on paper or directly on the potato is not in the true nature of potato printing.

Be careful when you cut out corners and points in the design. It's easy to make the wrong cut on a crisp potato. This part is most easily done with a linoleum cutter, but be sure to wipe off well after use. Get all the potato moisture off the cutter.

A potato shrinks quickly so you can't use it to print with over a long period of time. You can, however, save it for a few days if you rinse it thoroughly and keep it in a tight plastic bag in the refrigerator.

You can also combine potato printing with linoleum block printing. If you think you need to add a small rectangle or triangle in a linoleum-block design, you can very quickly and easily make a potato print to use.

If you are planning to do a lot of potato printing, or if children are working at this, it's a good idea to cover the entire table top with newspaper and brown paper.

This deeply serrated knife is a kitchen knife used to cut fluted slices of carrots. It is also good for making potato prints.

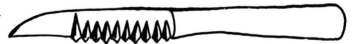

MATCHBOXES WITH POTATO PRINTING

Potato printing provides numerous possibilities for decorative use of both paper and material. You can make borders and patterns

8

on book covers for textbooks, decorate placecards, greeting cards, paper napkins for a child's party, and gift packages and paper. Here we have selected large kitchen matchboxes and a cigarette container to decorate.

Select a box that has as little warping or rippling as possible. Get a flat top surface. The cigarette container is a cardboard cylinder. You can make a bottom with two pieces of tape crossed over the bottom.

Use quite heavy absorbent paper cut to size to fit the matchboxes. You will need four pieces: two for the top and bottom and two for the ends. For the cigarette container, you need one rectangular piece that fits all the way around the cylinder and laps over slightly.

When the print is dry you can glue it on the box using a good-quality hobby glue applied with a brush or spread on with a little piece of stiff bristle board.

The box at top left in the photograph was made with textile-

Bookmark printed with a carrot stamp. We used textile colors on coarse linen. In the center of the star we cut a square and printed the star pattern over the round background print, which is also a carrot stamp.

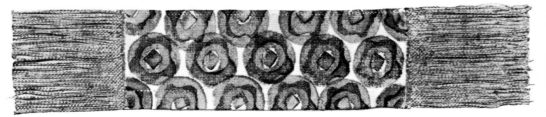

Background

A nature print with sectioned onions. Print the border with a carrot stamp. To the right is a test cloth for experimenting with onion prints. As a rule, chance decides the result of such natural printing. Play with the materials and placement.

printing colors printed on fabric. For the other two boxes, tempera was used on paper. Notice how an almost completely random and irregular pattern-cut becomes a decoration when you overprint. Here we used two tones of green.

CARROT PRINTING
You can use a carrot as a printing stamp instead of a potato. It's easy to work with, easy to cut into, and does not dry out as fast as a potato. Let the carrot dry for about half an hour, with the cut surface against newspaper, before you cut your design into it.

You can make a star pattern, as shown on page 9, in this way: Cut across a big firm carrot. Hollow it out a bit in the middle of the cut surface so you get a circle. Cut small points around the edge of the circle.

In the photograph on page 5 you will see a carrot cut out in this way, and on the paper on the table you can see prints made using the carrot design.

10

If you cut a length of carrot to about 2½ in. you can cut the same
star pattern in both the thin and thick ends of the carrot and then
print them inside each other. In the illustration on page 9 you can
see a small carrot pattern used on a bookmark. Two shades of the
same color were used.

You can also print stripes and plaids with cut carrots. The plaids
are made by printing the stripes on top of each other.

As you work with a technique and the materials, you will develop
ideas of your own and discover new possibilities.

NATURE PRINTING WITH ONIONS AND OTHER VEGETABLES

Not only the potato and the carrot can be used for printing.
Almost all vegetables can be used. Even a print made with an apple
cut in half with the core showing would be decorative by itself
without any further cutting. The more juice there is in the vegetable,
the more difficult it is to print with if you are using tempera. You
will have to use textile-print colors instead. You can reduce the
moisture, however, if you let the vegetables dry for about half an
hour with the cut surface placed against newspaper.

The lines in a sectioned onion are very decorative. You can cut
them lengthwise or crosswise. The onion needs no further cutting:
it makes its own design. The small rings inside the onion are likely
to fall out during the printing, however, so you may have to use
several onions if you are doing a large design. A few straight pins
pushed into the onion from the side will help to hold the onion
together. Print the patterns overlapping so the outlines are not too
definite. It is not easy to find two onions with the exact same pattern! A certain restraint is needed for this type of print; if not
handled with discrimination it may turn out looking commonplace
because there is no personal creativity behind the printing. We can
take our inspiration from nature, but we should not print nature
literally.

NEGATIVE AND POSITIVE PRINTING

In the prints we have been working with so far, the pattern has been
cut out to appear in *relief* on the potato or other vegetable stamp.
This way we got a print that is called *positive*, and it appears dark
on the white paper.

If, instead, you had hollowed out a figure in the potato, as shown
in the middle row, on page 12, the pattern would stand out as white
against a dark background, since it is not the pattern design that
prints but the surrounding portion. This print is called a *negative*
print.

11

It requires skill to cut complicated patterns in a potato. By the way, you can also cut patterns in beets!

To make a negative print, first sketch the border shape. That will show you the space you have to work in. Then sketch in the shape of the chosen pattern motif. Start with something easy, such as a triangle. Hollow out, working from the middle toward the contour line. The bobby pin (kirby grip) is excellent for this work. Finally, cut away the border or excess you don't want in the stamp frame. In the example shown the outside edges were cut away to make a square stamp.

Textile colors

Although the ready-mixed textile colors are somewhat more expensive than those you mix yourself, if you are working in a nursery school, senior citizens' home, or the like, it might be advantageous to use them.

You can use the colors directly from the jar, provided you add a fixing or setting agent to make the colors sun- and water-fast, so they won't fade or run. (It may not be necessary to add a fixing agent for some colors, but you must be prepared to have them fade eventually.)

If you do not want to print with pure, strong colors, you will have to lighten them with extender. If you are going to do all this, it may be just as easy to mix the colors from scratch. (There are countless books on the procedure for mixing these colors.)

Top row: Positive flower pattern cut in potato and used as a border. The striped pattern with the flowers is also a potato print.

Middle row: Negative pattern cut from square potato. Illustration shows a single print followed by several prints placed in various ways.

Bottom row: Alternating negative and positive patterns.

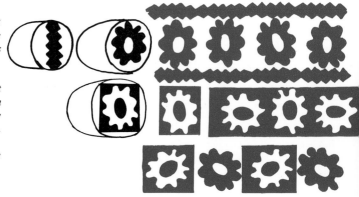

Many color products are available. We'll only mention a few, but that doesn't mean the others aren't as good. In choosing colors, avoid those that have a "sticky" consistency, which makes the print greasy and the fabric stiff. Textile colors come in basic colors that can be combined to make a variety of intermediate values and hues.

You can obtain water-based textile paints or oil-based inks. In both cases they come in transparent or opaque. Examples of such paints and inks are: Prang's Aquatex and Speedball inks. In Great Britain Reeves Fabric Dye for water based and Reeves Fabric Oil for oil based.

Making the inking pad

In using the potato or other vegetable stamp, the stamp itself is inked with a brush or piece of foam rubber. In printing with linoleum blocks, this method is not suitable. You must use an inking pad.

The inking pad is similar to the inking pad you get for rubber stamps. The principle for block printing is that you distribute the color on a piece of fabric with a flat brush like the one used for mixing colors (see below). This fabric is placed on top of the inking pad and the linoleum block is pressed into the color and then pressed on the fabric you are going to print. The inking pad assures an even and beautiful print.

Once in a while you will see a novice apply the color to the block with a brush. No professional textile printer will ever accept this procedure. The print will have a brush-stroke appearance and look "painted"—quite the opposite of the effect you want in textile printing. You may also easily get a grubby and dull print by applying color with a brush, since the color has a tendency to collect in

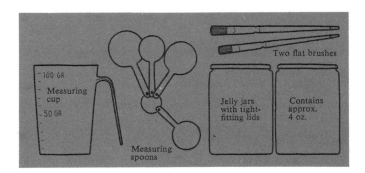

100 GR
Measuring cup
50 GR
Measuring spoons
Two flat brushes
Jelly jars with tight-fitting lids
Contains approx. 4 oz.

all the grooves and give a "false print." The results look amateurish. Don't use a piece of foam rubber either, because its porosity will produce small bubbles in the color, and they will appear on the print.

THE INKING PAD

Select a wooden board that will not warp. If you use an old cutting board that has become hollowed and worn, cover it with some cotton batting (sheeting).

Cut two pieces of ironing-board padding exactly the same size as the wooden board and place them on it.

Then place a piece of oilcloth on the table, cut off the corners, and turn the board with the padding, placing it in the middle (see diagram).

Tighten the oilcloth over the board and tack it in place with upholsterer's tacks ($\frac{7}{16}$ in. No. 4). Tack first along one side and then the other. Start tacking at the middle. Keep the oilcloth tight.

Fold in the corners and tack them in the same way. Finally, tighten the oilcloth over the two short ends and tack them. The back of the inking pad (the exposed wooden board) should be lacquered with enamel lacquer to prevent the moisture from soaking into the wood when you clean the pad.

USING THE INKING PAD AND THE TEST PRINT

The greatest difference between an inking pad for print-making and an ink pad for office use is that the color for the inking pad is applied to a small piece of fabric that you place on top of the pad. If you use maco (Egyptian cotton), avoid the kind that has a pattern woven in, since this will show up in the print.

Materials

Blockboard or fiberboard ($\frac{3}{8}$–1 in. thick). Choose size to suit your needs, for example, 8 in. × 12 in. Better too large than too small. Instead of this kind of board, you can use a rectangular cutting board that is not too thin.

A piece of ironing-board padding twice as large as the board.

A piece of oilcloth with a linen backing (not plastic) 4–5 in. wider and longer than the board.

Staples or upholsterers' tacks.

Clear enamel lacquer and a flat brush plus turpentine to clean the brush.

Making the inking pad. Place two pieces of ironing-board padding the same size as the board on the board, turn it over and place on the oilcloth. 1. Cut off the corners of the oilcloth. 2. Fold over one long side of the oilcloth and tack it to the board with tacks or staples. 3. Stretch the oilcloth tightly and then fold over the other long side and tack. Fold in the corners and bend the end pieces of the oilcloth in and tack them. Lacquer the exposed part of the board with the enamel lacquer.

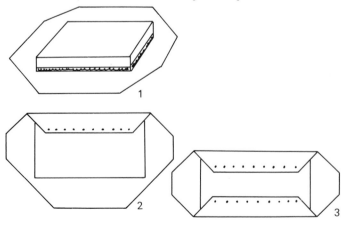

The piece of fabric that is called the inking cloth or simply "the cloth" should be a little larger than the block you plan to print with. If the cloth is much larger than the block it will consume unnecessary amounts of color and the cloth will also curl up and stick to the edge of the block.

Before you start a new inking pad, it is advisable to rub it with some dry scouring powder to make the cloth lie more securely.

Spread a covering layer of printing color on the inking pad, using the flat brush. Spread it on an area corresponding to the size of the inking cloth.

Place the cloth smoothly on top of the color, which will cause it to adhere to the pad.

Brush an even covering layer of color, not too thick, over the cloth including its edge, making sure the edge doesn't curl up.

Make a trial print with a potato stamp or linoleum block. The procedure is the same for either type. Press the block lightly down against the inking cloth two or three times, turning it 180 degrees between each pressure to insure that the color is evenly distributed on the stamp. Press down vertically but not too hard. Make sure that no color collects in the grooves of the block. If they fill up, the pattern will not make an imprint. Avoid color around the edge of the block, since this makes a "false print." Wipe off any excess color along the edge with a cloth. Now press the potato stamp or linoleum block against the fabric.

Read more about printing technique on page 30.

Read more about printing technique on page 30.

Materials
(In addition to paint and printing pad.)
One potato stamp or a linoleum block.
Scouring powder.
Leftover jersey material, flannel, or maco without a woven pattern.
A flat lacquer brush ($\frac{1}{2}$ in.), material or absorbent paper for trial print (blotting paper).
Newspaper.

Linoleum blocks

Since potato stamps don't last long and are not suitable for complicated patterns, linoleum blocks are usually preferred.

The technique is the same as for potato stamps: cut out a pattern, ink it, and print. Only the raised part makes the print and the print is a mirror image.

Linoleum is an excellent material to work with. It is easy to sketch on, easy to cut into, and gives a uniform print. Linoleum is also relatively inexpensive, and it is durable.

It is hard to hold a linoleum block while printing, so it should be glued to a wooden block base. Do this before cutting out the pattern. If you stick to standard sizes in linoleum blocks, you can buy them at modest prices already mounted on the wooden backing. This is the best for you if you are not accustomed to sawing, because these blocks must be very accurate.

If you do want a specially-sized block, then you will have to make your own.

15

LINOLEUM

Linoleum is a man-made product invented in 1860. The main ingredients are linseed oil, red-lead resin, and powdered cork.

Linoleum is built up of two layers. On top is the linoleum mixture and below a supporting layer of burlap; you can buy it in different thicknesses and qualities at hobby shops and art supply stores. You can get the ready-made linoleum blocks at hobby shops. In selecting unmounted linoleum, you should choose a heavy quality, brown, at least $\frac{1}{8}$ in. thick. The thicker the linoleum, the easier it is to cut. Linoleum that is worn from use on a floor or counter is not suitable. Vinyl and other plastics cannot be used.

HOMEMADE LINOLEUM BLOCKS

Materials
Linoleum for block.
Block or fiberboard, $\frac{3}{4}$ in. thick.
Saw.
Pencil, ruler, and perhaps a drafting triangle.
Sharp knife (utility knife, hunting knife, pocket or kitchen knife).
Sandpaper.
Hobby glue.
Brush or old table-knife to apply the glue.

If you prefer not to make your own blocks, skip these directions.

To make blocks, you glue the linoleum to a 20 in. × 20 in. blockboard and then saw out the sizes you will use. If you have to saw different shapes (not rectangular) it will be difficult to use a coping saw on a board this large and you must restrict yourself to a 5 in. × 20 in. board.

It is easiest to make several blocks while you are at it, and it's also very useful to have some spares. Make the board large enough so you can make a mistake and still have enough to get the desired number of blocks.

Cut a piece of linoleum in the same size as the board. Draw the outline on the linoleum with a pencil and cut down into the linoleum along the line, using a sharp knife. A metal ruler is a good guide to cut along. Cut down as far as you can into the linoleum. Bend it cautiously toward the back. Then cut the threads on the back. (Be sure to work on a surface you don't care about—an old wooden cutting board or worktable.)

Spread hobby glue (Bostik) on the board and on the back of the linoleum with a brush, an old knife, or spatula with a broad, pliable blade like a palette knife. Use the knife as you would in buttering a piece of bread. Press the two pieces together very firmly and hold in clamps for 24 hours. Use C-clamps to tighten the pieces, but be sure to put a smoothly planed piece of wood between the clamp and your linoleum block so you will not mar the surface.

Now you can saw the finished board into the desired linoleum-block sizes. Use a drafting triangle and T-square to check your corners and make sure they are at right angles. Sand the block with sandpaper or pencil-pointer (see pages 21–22).

The reason for mounting the block before cutting the pattern is to get the linoleum firmly glued to the wooden backing at all points.

If you cut the design first and then try to glue it to the block, it will be very hard to get all the areas to adhere firmly and you will have an uneven and bad printing job.

DRAWING A PATTERN ON THE BLOCK

To cut out a pattern you have previously drawn, the procedure is as follows:

Draw the pattern on tracing paper cut to the size of the block. Include the outline of the block on the tracing paper. If the pattern needs to be reversed when it is cut in the block, in order to get a right-reading print, you can reverse your pattern tracing by simply turning it over and drawing the pattern lines on the back of the tracing. Then use that side as your guide in cutting on the block. (It's easier to use a pattern that doesn't have to be reversed.)

Cut the tracing-paper with your drawing somewhat larger than the linoleum block, and cut a piece of carbon paper exactly the size of the block. Sand the linoleum to a matte (dull) finish with sand-paper, so it will take the drawing better. Place the carbon paper on the block with the carbon portion toward the linoleum. Place the tracing over the carbon. Smooth out the paper and tape it or thumbtack it to the sides of the block so it won't slip. Now transfer your design to the block by drawing along the lines with a ball-point pen.

Transfer the drawing precisely. This will provide your only guide lines for cutting. It is best to use a ruler for the straight lines.

If your lines do not come out clearly and distinctly on the block, go over them with pencil. Finally, draw crosshatch lines or diagonal lines in white-color pencil on the linoleum areas that are to be cut away, so you will not make any mistakes.

CUTTING THE BLOCK

In hobby shops, art shops, and paint stores where textile printing materials are sold, you may also be able to find linoleum cutter sets. Some are quite inexpensive, others are very expensive. The most common set consists of four to five cutters or nibs plus a handle. The cutters fit into the handle. Handles with a chuck for tightening are preferable, because they eliminate the risk of having the cutter slip or fall out while you are working. The best cutting sets have each cutter fastened into its own handle. An example is shown in the photograph.

Wood-carving tools are also excellent for linoleum-block work.

Each of the cutters has its own special profile and it is either V- or U-shaped. You will need both types.

17

Use the V-gouge to follow the outline. Use the U-gouge for the "dirty" work, that is, the cutting away of linoleum surfaces that are not going to be printed.

You can get both V- and U-shaped gouges in wide and narrow shapes. A good U-gouge for fine lines is now available in stores (see drawing). This tool can be partially substituted for a V-gouge.

Beginners find that these sharp tools and cutters slip easily. Therefore, **never hold your hand in front of the cutter in the cutting direction.** The wooden block will be helpful, because you can hold onto it while cutting. Practise on a test block first, before doing your first pattern, so you get the feel of the tools.

The principles for all cutting is as follows:

First cut lightly and then press more heavily. Cut up to the lines of the pattern, but do not cut them away. Cut almost down to the webbing, but avoid unraveling it. If you cut all the way down to the wood, you risk the chance that water will penetrate into it when you are cleaning the block. The water could loosen the linoleum from the block.

The edges of the pattern should be cut at steep angles away from the pattern, with curved or slanted sides as shown in the diagram on page 21. Avoid cutting underneath the pattern or the outline won't be pressed down and will not make sharp prints.

First follow the outline with the narrowest V-gouge. The shape

Cutting a block. Use the V-gouge close to the outline and the U-gouge for cutting away large areas.

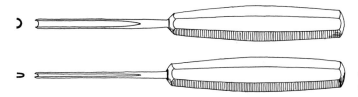

Background

Linoleum-block cutting set. The cutters and knives are screwed into the chuck handle at left.

Linoleum-block cutting set with loose cutters and handle.

V- and U-shaped wood-carving tools are excellent for linoleum blocks, especially the detail work.

of the cutter will naturally form the slant toward the pattern if you use it correctly. If you find it easier to make the cut edge vertical, this will be equally good if you are not cutting fine details that need a wide base to avoid breaking down in the pressure of printing.

After you have started the outline with the narrow V-gouge use a wider V-gouge and cut deeper. After that, use the wide U-gouge and cut away all the linoleum that you have cross-hatched in pencil. Check periodically to see that you have not left elevations in the bottom, since these might be high enough to show up in the print. Finally, cut the outlines clean with the narrow V-gouge and smooth out all the irregularities.

If you have a utility knife, it will be useful for scoring the straight pattern lines, cutting along a metal ruler.

Cut the bottom smooth and even.

The cutting is very important for a good print, so you must be extremely careful.

If you happen to cut into the pattern—and this can easily happen to a beginner—you need not throw the block out. Keep it and see if you can work out another design that will eliminate the mistake. See the example in the diagram on page 21. See page 79 for more on cutting mistakes.

GENERAL RULES FOR CUTTING

1. Keep the hand that supports the block away from the direction in which you are cutting.

2. First cut close to the outline. If the pattern is positive, cut outside the drawing line. If it is negative, cut inside the drawing line. Use the V-gouge.

3. Cut out any fine points in a pattern by cutting *away* from the shape. When you are at the bottom of the corner or notch, cut away the last of the linoleum—still against the angle. For this, you can also use a pocket knife or utility knife to make the corner completely clean.

4. Always cut lightly first—then more heavily.

5. Cut away everything that must be removed, using the U-gouge.

6. Cut so that the edge of the pattern stands either vertically (perpendicular to the base) or, in the case of very fine details, beveled.

7. If necessary, cut everything clean with the narrow V-gouge.

8. Do not cut into the burlap (hessian) backing.

FINISHING THE BLOCK AND MAKING A TRIAL PRINT

When you have cut the block, make a trial print (see pages 29–30). If the print is not satisfactory because it shows off parts of the block that were not supposed to print, clean the color off the block with soap and water, using a medium-soft nail brush. Make the necessary corrections. If the test print is satisfactory, make a print on sturdy paper, such as brown paper. When the print is dry, cut to the same size as the block; glue it on the back of the block with hobby glue, exactly as the print should look. This way you can always see what is up and what is down on the block and you can position the block correctly. A glued-on print is much safer than an arrow or direction line on the back of the block.

When the glue is dry, lacquer the block on the back and sides with floor varnish or clear cellulose lacquer. Clean the brush with turpentine if you use varnish. If you use cellulose lacquer clean the brush with thinner. It takes several hours for varnish to dry, but it is harder than cellulose lacquer, which dries in about 20 minutes. If lacquered, the block is easy to clean when it has been used, and it will not be damaged by water.

If you happened to expose the burlap while cutting the pattern, lacquer the place immediately—after first brushing off the block and cleaning any dust from the area you intend to lacquer.

Finally, sand the printing surface of the plate with emery cloth. If you are tempted to omit this sanding—don't!

To avoid spoiling fine points and details while you cut out the block, follow the correct direction for cutting.

20

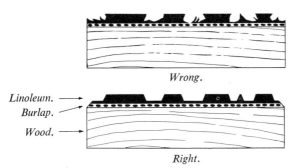

Wrong.

Linoleum. →
Burlap. →
Wood. →

Right.

Background

The raised parts of the block must have clean, beveled, or completely vertical edges and the bottom must be even and free of shreds, shavings, and dust.

Don't throw away a block with a mistake. Use it for another pattern. At left: We made a chip in the triangle and changed the block to a new pattern. At right: *We made a new pattern out of the chipped quadrangle.*

When it is sanded, the block will take the color better, since linoleum is a greasy material and has a tendency to repel the paint. Sandpaper can be used instead of emery cloth, but the cloth is more durable; if you make a sanding board, the sanding process takes practically no time. If the block won't take color even after sanding, wipe if off with acetone or press it against the inking pad and rub it off firmly on a newspaper. You may need to repeat this several times. When you sand, remember to do it over paper or a wastepaper basket.

The finishing process for very large blocks is described on page 81.

If the linoleum is very hard, place the block briefly on a radiator or close to heat. Don't leave it too long or it will warp.

SANDING BLOCK AND PENCIL-POINTER
Buy a sheet of emery cloth 9 in. × 11 in. Cut out a piece 6 in. × 8 in. and glue it on a piece of planed wood, blockboard, or fiberboard. Use hobby glue.

Then rub the printing block evenly on this sanding block to dull the surface, but without rounding off edges and corners. Don't use the sanding block as a file. It is the *printing block* that you must move back and forth *over* the sanding block, not vice versa.

You can make a pencil-pointer from the leftovers and use it for sanding raw edges of the wooden block. Get a wide paint stirrer (see picture on page 22) and glue emery cloth on both sides. You can, of course, use emery cloth without gluing it to a surface, but it is easier to work if it is glued down on a firm support.

FLOCKING
There is nothing to prevent you from printing with the linoleum block as it is now, but if you want a clean, sharp, perfect print you really should take the trouble to flock the block (see note at end of this section).

If you make prints next to each other, one with a flocked block and one with an unflocked block, you will easily see the difference.

Materials
Paper in thickness and quality
 of writing paper.
Hobby glue.
Varnish or clear cellulose
 lacquer and a small brush,
 turpentine or thinner.
A watercolor brush or a brush
 such as a toothbrush.
Emery cloth.
Acetone, possibly.

21

Top: *A sanding block.* Bottom: *A pencil-pointer. Both are homemade. The abrasive is emery cloth.*

The print from the unflocked block appears dull and dreary and even mottled next to the full and beautifully-covering print of the flocked block.

Flock only after you have lacquered the block and have let it dry completely. Otherwise you risk lacquer rising on top of the flocking. (Clean the brush in turpentine.)

After this, paint all the raised areas of the block, that is, the parts that will print, with the slow-drying white enamel lacquer.

Put the flocking in the strainer and shake it out in an even layer over a glass plate or piece of cardboard. While the lacquer is still wet, press the block against the flocking so that the flocking adheres to the block.

Let the block dry for at least 48 hours and then brush off the loose flocking. If there is any flocking in the cut-out areas, you must clean it out with a cutting tool. Finally, polish the edges of the block with the sanding board.

It is less effective to sprinkle the flocking directly from the strainer onto the lacquered surface of the plate. You get the most even layer by dabbing the block against the flocking.

If you use the block often the flocking will eventually wear off. Then you must sand the surface clean with the sanding block and repeat the flocking process.

Make sure you buy wool flocking, not nylon flocking, since the latter makes an inferior print.

Blocks that you use for background printing (blocks without pattern to make solid color areas) should also be flocked. Never use unflocked and flocked blocks for the same work. The difference in the prints will be too apparent.

Background flocks can be flocked by using adhesive drawer-lining with a felt surface, such as is used for silver drawers.

Cut the drawer-lining very carefully to the size of the block and place it on the block. If the piece is too large, sand it down to size with the emery-cloth block after you have attached it to the block. When the first layer wears down, put a new one on. Remember, this method is only for blocks without a pattern.

NOTE: The appearance of a print will also depend on the consistency of the textile color and the quality of the color band. If you are going to print with ready-mixed colors you should not normally flock the block since these colors yield a more "gooey" print and flocking increases this. In this case, the block is ready for printing after sanding is finished.

Flocking the finished block. First paint the surface with slow-drying white enamel lacquer, then dab it against the flocking dust that has been strained onto an even surface, such as a glass plate. A flocked block gives a much handsomer imprint than an unflocked one.

A modular block system

Even though you have cut a block for a certain use, it is quite certain that you'll use it later in a completely different work. From the illustrations in this book, you'll discover that several of our blocks have been reused in other works.

In order to use them with each other successfully, they must fit into a system where the dimensions match—such a system is called a modular system.

Module is the name for a base measure from which other measures can be derived. Within building construction, the modular system is used widely, and it makes it possible to design prefabricated construction elements that fit together harmoniously.

For this book we have worked out a basic modular system consisting of a series of mounted linoleum blocks that match each other.

Materials
Slowly drying white enamel lacquer.
Small brush and turpentine.
Flocking.
Glass plate, cardboard lid, or some other even surface.
Fine strainer (see photograph).
Small bristle brush.

An unflocked block gives a mottled and uninteresting print. However, normally you do not flock the block when using ready-made colors.

23

Background   The base for the system is the square block A. It measures
1⅜ in. × 1⅜ in. B is two times A. C is three times A. D is six times,
H four times, F eight times. You can make your own modular
system in this way to suit your need (see captions).

Blocks E, G, I, and K are "border" blocks matching the others.
L is a very useful small block—a quarter the size of the A block and
it can be used in corner patterns, in borders with the other border
blocks.

Block M falls a bit outside the family, since it is a parallelogram
(rhombus), but its long diagonal corresponds to the side of the A
block.

The square and rectangular blocks have many uses, but you may
also need blocks with other shapes, such as triangular. For this
purpose we worked out the system shown in the illustrations on
this page. Several of these blocks can be combined with the modular system, as you can see from the dimensions.

To begin with, you should use just two or three of the blocks.
Blocks A and H are extremely useful. It is wisest to begin with
square blocks.

(These blocks are available ready-made in Denmark and can be
ordered simply by the letter and number. Suppliers are: A/S
Schjerning, Lykkesholmsallé 20, Copenhagen V, Denmark; and
Kaj Verner Christensen, Ole Jørgensgade 13, Copenhagen N,
Denmark.)

If you are making your own modular system of blocks, you must
be extremely careful to get the dimensions exact, otherwise the
work is as good as wasted. The blocks shown in this modular system
are used for almost all the models in the book.

Printing table and padding for block printing

Your printing table must be steady and have an even surface. It
should be placed in front of a window so you can judge the colors
in daylight. For evening work, the source of light must be good. A
desk or drafting lamp that you can move around in all directions is
good.

The table must be large enough for the fabric on which you are
planning to print, as well as for all your work tools. Keep these to
the right of the material.

Put the inking pad, colors, and brushes on a little tray by themselves to avoid spotting the material or anything else.

Keep the colors and brushes next to the inking pad to avoid lift-
ing a full brush over the other materials. It might drip, you know!

Always cover the material that you are not working on with white
paper or newspaper to avoid spotting.

24

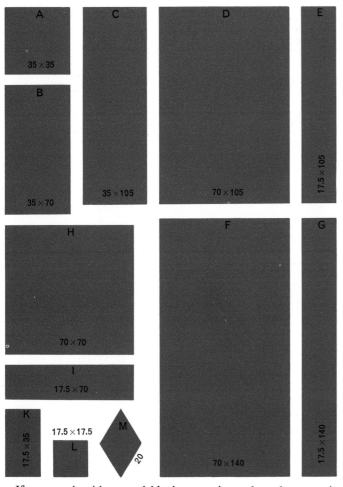

The dimensions of this modular system of blocks are such that the smaller fit into the larger. The basic block is block A, a square, 35 × 35 millimeters. The other blocks are derived from A. Block M is a rhombus and looks different but fits into the system since its long diagonal measures 35 mm. NOTE: *The measurements are shown in millimeters to accurately represent the Danish system. A conversion table to decimal inches appears below for those who wish to make this system themselves. Fractional inches are not accurate enough to make the blocks fit perfectly.*

Conversion Table

Millimeters	Inches	
	decimal (accurate to 0.001)	fractional (only approx.)
17.5	0.689	$\frac{11}{16}$
20	0.787	$\frac{25}{32}$
35	1.378	$1\frac{3}{8}$
70	2.756	$2\frac{3}{4}$
105	4.134	$4\frac{1}{8}$
140	5.512	$5\frac{1}{2}$

If you work with several blocks at a time, place those not in immediate use on a tray or piece of cardboard, with the patterns up.

Pad the printing section of the table with an ironing board pad or wool blanket without holes or other bumps. Make sure this is very smooth. Stretch a clean piece of linen over this and fasten with thumbtacks or tape underneath the table.

It is useful to draw a grid with a 2 in. to 3 in. square on the linen covering at the top, along one or both sides. This will enable you to position the prints properly.

Instead of a table you could use a sheet of thick plywood or blockboard, 20 in. × 28 in. covered in the same way.

25

Blocks in a system of triangles. Several of the blocks fit into the modular system. The measurements are shown in millimeters. Conversion table below gives inches in decimals accurate enough to fit the Danish modular system. (Fractional measurements are only approximate.)

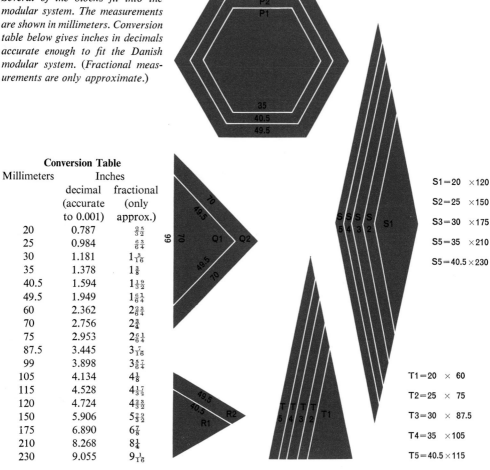

Conversion Table

Millimeters	Inches decimal (accurate to 0.001)	fractional (only approx.)
20	0.787	$\frac{2}{3}\frac{5}{2}$
25	0.984	$\frac{6}{6}\frac{3}{4}$
30	1.181	$1\frac{3}{16}$
35	1.378	$1\frac{3}{8}$
40.5	1.594	$1\frac{19}{32}$
49.5	1.949	$1\frac{61}{64}$
60	2.362	$2\frac{23}{64}$
70	2.756	$2\frac{3}{4}$
75	2.953	$2\frac{61}{64}$
87.5	3.445	$3\frac{7}{16}$
99	3.898	$3\frac{57}{64}$
105	4.134	$4\frac{1}{8}$
115	4.528	$4\frac{17}{32}$
120	4.724	$4\frac{23}{32}$
150	5.906	$5\frac{29}{32}$
175	6.890	$6\frac{7}{8}$
210	8.268	$8\frac{1}{4}$
230	9.055	$9\frac{1}{16}$

S1 = 20 ×120

S2 = 25 ×150

S3 = 30 ×175

S5 = 35 ×210

S5 = 40.5 ×230

T1 = 20 × 60

T2 = 25 × 75

T3 = 30 × 87.5

T4 = 35 ×105

T5 = 40.5 ×115

26

BASIC PRINCIPLES

Printing with color: doilies (napkins)

Making doilies is a quick and easy way to practise the elementary techniques.

Varying patterns, colors, and methods of printing the doilies will give you a good foundation experience on which to build.

THE MATERIAL
Use muslin or poplin that has been thoroughly washed to remove all the sizing. If you print on material with sizing, the print will simply disappear with the sizing the first time you wash the material.

After washing the material, iron it carefully to remove any creases. If a piece of fabric has fold or crease marks you run the risk of your print not "taking" on these areas.

Cut out in 7 in. × 7 in. squares for the doilies. This includes room for the border, hems, and fringes.

THE BLOCKS
Use two 1⅜ in. × 1⅜ in. blocks corresponding to modular block A·
Cut a pattern only in one but flock both blocks.

Cut a reasonably simple geometric design in the pattern block.

Textile printing is a craft that demands dexterity with a tool, especially cutting tools. In order to learn this it is important that you do not start off with difficult tasks. It is always easiest to cut geometrical patterns with straight lines, such as the ones shown. Start with a negative pattern. You will then have the imprints of the sides of the block to guide the following printings.

If you use a positive pattern, it should touch all four sides of the block so you can place the next print correctly. On page 32 there are some examples of positive patterns suitable for square blocks.

Note that the entire surface of the block is used on the figures shown. If a positive pattern is located in the middle of a block it will be difficult to print with it since it is not easy to place it precisely (see also the drawing of the potato print on page 7). Draw some patterns yourself according to this principle.

You can use graph paper to sketch on. Avoid small details; they are difficult to cut.

MARKING THE MATERIAL

Place the prints precisely on the doilies by first finding the middle of each doily. You can proceed in one of several ways. You could use a pencil very lightly, but the lines might remain when the material is heat treated. So this method is not so good. It is better to make folds in the material, twice to make a cross, dividing it into four equal parts. The fold must not be too sharp and not ironed in, only pressed down with a fingernail. If the crease is too sharp it will show up in the print because the material becomes uneven and won't take color there. A third method is to use a stylus to cautiously scratch lines on the material. The stylus can be the blunt end of an orange stick, a bone letter-opener, a folding stick or paper folder such as bookbinders use. It is most important that it have a dull end. If you press too hard the marks could show up in the print.

Finally, mark the outline of the pattern with a basting thread but do not print over the thread. Some textile printers use threads

This doily has a very simple but decorative triangular pattern. The procedure here differs somewhat from that described in the text. Use a ruler as a guide to keep the triangular blocks straight. Stretch out the material on the printing board, using straight pins. We used two linking cloths with different colors and kept the colors in small glass jars properly labeled. Drops from the brushes will fall into the lids if placed as in the photograph.

28

Easy negative blocks. Negative patterns are easiest to start with since the sharply delineated four-sided color surface makes it easier to place the next print. The straight pattern lines are easy to cut, and it is easy to create new patterns according to this principle.

stretched between two straight pins, but this technique will probably appear too cumbersome for most beginners. Folding the material or marking with a stylus are recommended.

STRETCHING THE MATERIAL, THE TEST PRINT

Save a piece of the material for a test print, or you could use one doily (napkin) for this.

Stretch the material along the grain on the printing table, using straight pins at the corners and in the middle of each side. Put the pins in at an angle from the outside so they will not get in the way of the printing. Also watch out for raw edges and loose threads under the material. Tape can also be used for mounting the fabric.

At the same time, smooth out any folds so they are only faintly visible and won't interfere with the printing.

Use two inking cloths for the inking pad when you use two colors. Start with the uncut background block.

Brush one color on the inking pad to cover an area corresponding to the inking cloth (it is a bit larger than the block). Put the inking cloth on this color; it will adhere. Then paint the color on the

29

Basic Principles

inking cloth and a little bit beyond the edges to prevent it from sliding and curling up.

Dab the block vertically down on the inking cloth (not too hard) between each print. Lightly dab an extra time while turning the block 180 degrees to assure an even distribution of color on the block. Always dab in the same way each time so the prints will appear uniform in color. Check to see that the inking cloth is smooth every time you dab.

Now press the inked block down against the material that is stretched out on the table, keeping the block vertical. Work at each print with the same pressure so that the result will be a beautiful, uniform print. It's best to stand up while printing since this way it is easier to aim and position the prints precisely.

Be careful with the colors. If you dab against the inking pad at an angle or if the block hasn't been completely saturated with paint, it will immediately show up in the printing. Check constantly to make sure that there is no accumulation of color along the edges of the block, since this will cause a dark frame around the print. Wipe off the excess paint along the edge with a rag. A single "false print" can spoil a project.

Before you really launch into your project, try several print experiments. Even if you are experienced, make these test prints. You can use both light and dark colors and in several tones. First print with the unpatterned or background block. Then, when the color is dry, overprint with the patterned block. Use light and dark colors with the unpatterned blocks and try two printings in different colors, one on top of the other. During these experiments try to position the prints exactly next to each other, so you will learn how to do this precisely. Use a fold in the fabric or a ruler as a guide. If you use a ruler or wooden molding as a guide, remember to weight it down with something heavy at the end to prevent its moving between prints.

It doesn't help to repeat the printing if it turns out too light. Regardless of how light a print is, a double print will always look darker than the remaining single prints.

PRINTING THE DOILY (NAPKIN)
The doily at right on page 32: stretch the fabric on the board in the same way as you stretched the test cloth.

Start in the middle with the four background block prints. Position these prints around the center cross formed by the folds. Position the prints precisely so you do not get white canals or lines between the prints or overprints by overlapping the prints, which will show up as a dark line when the project is finished.

Materials
Printing table or printing board.
Flat brush for mixing or stirring paint.
Inking pad with two inking cloths (one for each shade), two modular blocks A, 1⅜ in × 1⅜ in. (one with cut pattern and both possibly flocked).
Material (muslin or poplin), 7 in. × 7 in. for each doily plus a leftover for test print.
Textile colors.
Small bowl with damp cloth or sponge to clean your fingers.
Straight pins, scissors, and measuring tape.

30

When you have completed the four background block prints, print the frame around these with a pattern block. Print the frame by placing the blocks precisely around the center print. This makes a total of eight prints with the patterned block. Save the corners till last, and be careful in doing them to avoid canals or overprint lines. Now you will have 12 blocks in the frame. The doily at left (page 32) uses the same blocks. Four printings of the pattern block form the center design. Twelve printings of the background block make the dark border.

More about doilies (napkins) on page 36.

CLEANING BLOCKS AND OTHER MATERIALS

Wash the paint off the blocks with cold water, soap, and a nail brush. Brush lightly with the nail brush and wipe lightly with a rag. Remember to wear your apron while cleaning.

Paint has a tendency to harden around the inking cloth on the inking pad if you have been working for a long time, so water and soap won't do the cleaning job. Then you'll have to rub with scouring powder and rinse with cold water.

Old, stubborn paint can be removed with the following mixture:

	Weight (mass) ratio	Fluid (volume) ratio
Benzene (petroleum, ether)	9	4
Gasoline (petrol)	9	5
Ethyl alcohol (denatured alcohol)	2	1

(In grams this is 45 grams benzene, 45 grams gasoline, and 10 grams alcohol.)

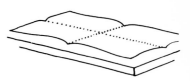

Place the material on the printing table with the back of the folds down. If the material is turned with the fold marks up they may leave white lines in the print. The folds are exaggerated in this drawing for clarification.

If there is a thread on the material when you print it, will be visible as a printing error in the finished work.

Two easy doilies you can make with only 16 printings. Be careful in using a dark color toward the center with a light border, since the dark will dominate and impair the overall impression. Both doilies are printed with the same blocks.

Three examples of easy positive blocks with the patterns cut to the edge so you can place neighboring prints precisely without white stripes or overlappings. The edge drawn around the patterns was made only to show the extent of the blocks. Don't cut the edges out in the pattern. The edges do not appear in the pattern.

Rub on this mixture with a rag. Warning: It is very flammable.

Clean the brushes completely by rubbing them against your palm, using soap and water.

Some people are allergic to paint and should avoid contact with it. Use rubber gloves (the thin, disposable plastic gloves are less suitable as they do not fit tightly).

Heat setting

To make the textile paints mentioned in this book color fast in water and sunshine, you must set the colors. This goes for prints with ready-made colors or homemade colors. Heat sets colors without changing their appearance.

You can do this thermal or heat setting of color in several ways: (1) by ironing, (2) by heating in an oven, and (3) by treating with an electric mangle.

Regardless of the method, the setting must not be done until 24 hours after printing. Otherwise you risk having the paint rub off during the process. Do not use a higher temperature than the material can take. (See pages 40–42 about setting material with several overprints.)

SETTING WITH AN IRON

This method is only suitable for small items because it is so slow. Put tissue paper or old newspaper over and under the material to prevent the paint from smearing or rubbing off on the iron and ironing board. Don't use newspaper with colored pictures or print since this will rub off, unlike regular black newspaper ink. Do not use new newspapers, either, because fresh ink may rub off.

32

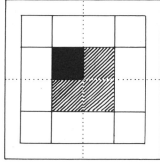 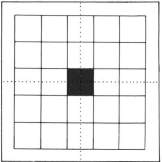

When you print a doily and similar small projects start in the middle around the folded center cross when there are an even number of prints in each direction. With an odd number of prints, start at the center directly on top of the cross. For an accurate positioning of the print, it is important that the block is marked at the middle on each side.

The iron should be heated to about 250 °F. Move it to assure that each and every square inch of the material has been treated for three minutes total. If the material can take it, use a higher temperature. For each 36 °F. you can reduce the time about one minute. Keep the printed side of the fabric down.

SETTING IN A BAKING OVEN

Smooth out the fabric on the table, over tissue paper, old newspaper, or clean cloth. Fold the paper around the fabric at one end and roll fabric and paper loosely together. All fabric must be covered by the paper everywhere so the color won't rub off onto other parts of the fabric, but don't roll it too tightly, otherwise the inner layers may not reach the desired temperature. When you have finished roll an extra piece of paper around the roll. Do not stuff any of this paper in at the ends since that would prevent heat

You cannot always tell whether a pattern is positive or negative. In this case, it is easy to place the next prints above or below the first one, but it is somewhat more difficult at the sides. The lines at the right and left do not belong to the pattern but only indicate the extent of the pattern block.

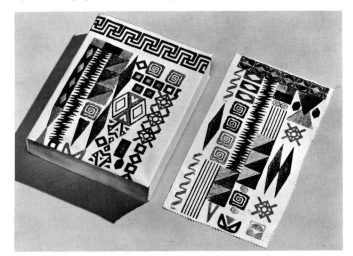

The trial cloths often turn out to be very decorative. The one at the left has been used as the cover for a large book. Trial cloths are good reminders of colors and patterns when you no longer have the original object and want to print a similar print.

33

Start a notebook from the very beginning of your work. Write up the color recipes and mixtures used in trial prints. When you lighten colors and mix your own colors, put samples in the notebook for future reference, even if it is not the final color you use. This way you can later reconstruct the color if you want it. Also insert pattern sketches and notes on the amount and type of fabric you used, and the price.

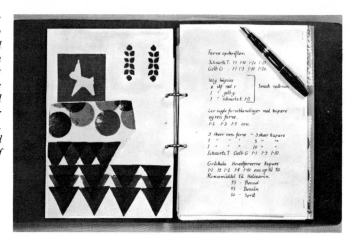

Never dry the cleaned blocks on radiators, registers, or the like, or they will warp.

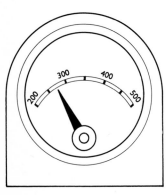

An oven thermometer for baking ovens without thermostat control. It is important to know the exact temperature of the oven since the heat setting requires definite time and temperature.

circulation. Keep the ends open. If the roll is very thick you must set it twice. The second time, roll the material in the opposite direction so the inside becomes the outside.

Heat the oven to 250 °F. and put the material on a clean baking sheet. The roll must not be so large that you will have to bend the material.

The setting takes 10 minutes at 250 °F.

If you use a gas oven, it is most practical to heat it to 300 °F., turn off the gas, and put the roll in.

If there is no thermostat control on the oven use an oven thermometer.

SETTING WITH AN ELECTRIC MANGLE
Paper is also used for this process, as with the oven, but make sure the material gets equal heat treatment everywhere. Every square inch must get at least four minutes between the rollers. The printed side must not face the heating element.

SETTING OF MATERIALS THAT CAN'T TAKE BOILING
Treat these materials with one of the above methods at 230 °F. for a scant five minutes.

SETTING LARGE OBJECTS
Send large items to a laundry or a dyeworks that sets colors. Check with them about the proper procedure.

WASHING AND DRY CLEANING
Be careful the first few times you wash prints made with water-based

34

paints, unless the paints are acrylic or polymer. Materials painted with black and red colors should be washed in lukewarm water the first two or three times, preferably with soap flakes, and not rubbed too hard.

Dry cleaning is not advisable. Some cleaners offer special handling, but be cautious.

Printed suede and chamois should not be heat set. They can't take washing or dry cleaning, either; they require special treatment. Check with your cleaner.

Positive and negative cutting for block printing

The principal difference between positive and negative patterns was discussed in the section on potato printing (pages 11–12). In both these print methods, only the raised part of the block prints. If you create a raised pattern by cutting away its surroundings, you get a positive print. If you cut away the pattern and leave the surroundings, you get a negative print.

The effect of the two types of prints is very different, and the interaction between positive and negative patterns is one of the most important artistic devices available to the textile printer. Along with the pattern and colors, the distribution between light and dark is important for the overall impression of the finished work; in this way you can make it appear closed or open, heavy or thin, light or dark, covering, or not covering.

The difference between the effects of the two printing methods is shown in the illustrations on page 37. We have chosen fish for this demonstration instead of geometrical patterns, since it will probably be easier to conceive the different possibilities this way. Exactly the same possibilities exist with clean geometrical patterns.

Figure 1 shows two fish. They are cut into the block so that the print is positive. The reproduction is the same as if you had drawn the fish on a piece of paper with a pencil or drafting pen.

Figure 2 shows the same two fish, but here the reproduction method has been reversed. What is black on drawing 1 is white here, and vice versa. The block is cut to make a negative print.

These two reproduction methods are the most common and they are the methods most often used by beginners. A skilled pattern-cutter can enrich the motif by combining positive and negative printing. Such combinations are shown in the following three drawings.

35

Figure 3 shows the bodies of the fish reproduced positive and the body markings negative (compare with drawing 1).

Figure 4 shows the fish bodies negative with the markings positive (compare with drawing 2).

Figure 5 shows a sophisticated combination of the last two reproduction methods (drawing 3 and 4). The block is divided into two portions. The upper half is dominated by the light color and the lower by the dark. The dark half will appear heavier and is therefore positioned at the bottom of the design. We get a certain balance between top and bottom, light and dark, by letting the light area be somewhat larger than the dark one.

You can obtain good effects with fabric printing if you alternate positive and negative blocks. You can also alternate a background print and a pattern print.

If you want to cover the pattern area with a color you can start off with a background print, and print over this with a positive block. Or you can use a block with a delicate negative pattern so that only the pattern will stand out on the color of the fabric as a light decoration. This will give the effect of a paint-covered material. More about this at the end of the next section.

We cannot give definite rules about using positive and negative prints, but the possibilities and combinations are tremendous.

More about doilies (napkins) and fabric printing

Because doilies are small and allow you to see the whole project as you work on it, you will be inspired to experiment with various design combinations. You can return again and again to the doilies and use them as test cloths for your own patterns.

With the earlier instructions as reference, we'll just sum up some of the variations illustrated on page 39.

1. Background prints in the middle and a patterned border in the same color around it.

2. The use of another color for the pattern edge—either a shade of the middle section or a different color entirely.

3. Overprint the entire doily with a patterned block—you might change colors for the border print.

4. Print as for illustration 3 but use two different pattern blocks alternately. Use one or two colors.

5. Print the entire doily with a background block. When this print is dry, in about half an hour, you can overprint with a patterned block on every other background print—either using the same color to get a darker shade in the pattern, or with another darker color such as black.

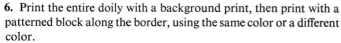

1. *Positive pattern.*

2. *Negative pattern.*

3. *Combination of positive and negative patterns. The bodies are in positive. The markings are negative.*

4. *Combination of positive and negative patterns. The bodies are negative and the markings positive.*

5. *A combination of printing techniques from figs. 3 and 4. The lower half with dark background could look heavy, but the picture has a balance because the upper section with a light background is made somewhat larger than the lower one.*

6. Print the entire doily with a background print, then print with a patterned block along the border, using the same color or a different color.

7. Print every other square with a background block and the remaining squares with a pattern block.

8. Print the entire doily with a repeat block so the whole surface will be covered by a continuous pattern (perhaps over a background print in the same or a different color).

There are many more possibilities for combinations. It pays to search for them. Use your imagination!

FOUR DOILIES (NAPKINS) MADE IN A DIFFERENT WAY

The doilies illustrated on page 41 differ from those described above. First of all, the number of prints differ. There is an odd number of prints on each side—five across, as opposed to the earlier four across. This means that you cannot print around the folded center cross.

Positioning of the prints: Cut out the doilies as before, 7 in. × 7 in.

Basic Principles

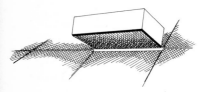

plus extra material for hems and fringe—the dimensions given are for the printing area only. Fold these doilies as before. Here the similarity ends. This time the first print must be placed exactly *over* the middle of the cross as shown in the drawing on page 33.

You will find it helpful to mark the middle of each block on all four sides and draw intersecting lines from these points (see pages 33 and 71).

After the first print, print out to both sides. Then print two rows exactly underneath the first prints, starting from the left. (Opposite if you are left-handed.)

Turn the doily 180 degrees and print the remaining two rows in the same way. If you use a background block, the resulting 25 squares must form one square—and sides must be as completely straight as if drawn by a ruler.

The doilies shown on page 41 were first printed with a background block as described.

TIPS ABOUT PRINTING ERRORS

Correcting mistakes in the background print: If by mistake you have placed a print with the background block so that a white line forms between one print and the next print, you can repair the damage by tipping the background block very cautiously up against the white line as shown in the drawing. Normally there will be enough paint on the edge of the block to cover the white line. It is *very risky* to dab the block against the inking pad again and then print on the white line since usually you will pick up so much paint that the repair will look like an overprint.

Such a line in the print indicates that the block print is a hairbreadth off. If the repair is successful, you can make an adjustment in the next row when you print the square underneath. Just place a "mask" (absorbent paper) on the fabric so that a hairline at the bottom will print on the absorbent paper rather than on the material. This will prevent overprinting.

The colors: It is best to buy the three basic colors first: blue, yellow, and red, plus black. With these you can mix many other colors. You might prefer to use mixed colors for these doilies.

Red and yellow make orange. Between the red and yellow colors are many orange shades that you can get by mixing the proportions to your liking—using varying amounts of the base colors.

Blue and yellow make green. Blue and red make violet. Red and blue are especially difficult to mix and the result is often a muddy

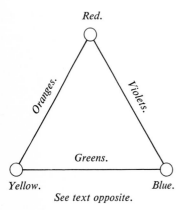

Red.

Oranges.

Violets.

Greens.

Yellow.

Blue.

See text opposite.

38

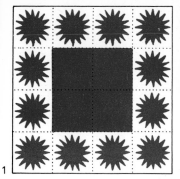

1

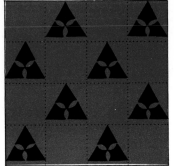

Even the small format of doilies offers rich possibilities for variation in design. A doily with 16 squares is used here to indicate the varied design possibilities. (An interesting set of ready-made stamps are tree stamps available at architectural and engineering suppliers. They might be used as in figs. 1 and 2.)

5

2

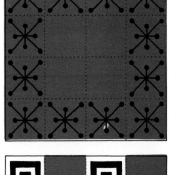

6

3

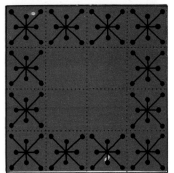

7

4

8

color due to the special pigments in the textile paints. It is best to buy a ready-made purple.

Lighten the colors with an extender or subdue them with a trifle, just a dab, of black.

When you mix colors start with the lightest color and add the deeper color until you obtain the desired color value.

Use measuring spoons to mix your colors and write down the amounts used, so you can make the same shade later on if you like it or need to match it.

The patterns: Geometric patterns are the easiest to draw and to cut. They also offer the richest number of possibilities for use and they create a harmonious pattern on the material.

DOILY (NAPKIN) I—OVERPRINT

For this doily use only one color. The chessboard pattern appears when you overprint every other square. As mentioned earlier, the shade appears darker when you overprint with the same color.

Use modular block A for the background print. The small squares in the light areas are printed with modular block L, with no pattern. Both blocks must be flocked.

You could also print this doily in two colors—light and dark.

DOILY (NAPKIN) II—OVERPRINT PATTERN WITH BORDER

Use the same blocks as for Doily I (modular blocks A and L) but use two colors. Make the border and pattern overprint with a darker color.

First print the five rows of five squares each that make the background print. Then, while the background print dries, print the border in the darker color, using modular block L.

Since modular block L is half as wide as block A, there will be 10 imprints along each side for the border plus one imprint in each of the four corners. Make the corner imprints last, after the remainder of the border has been printed.

Now print the pattern on top of the background print, again using block A. Aim for the very fine line pattern resulting from the background print (where the squares meet each other). The result is a kind of "double overprint" because new darker squares appear where the squares of the middle motif overlap. You can also obtain this effect with only one color.

Since the textile paints are transparent, you obtain an optical mixing of the colors when two different colors are overprinted.

Don't make too many overprints, however, otherwise the print will feel too "thick." We used three here: that is enough. The

1

2

3

4

The four very different doilies are described in the text. Patterns originally created for doilies can often be used for other larger projects. The unprinted white edge around the pattern should be in scale with the size of the overall pattern area.

material will also easily "burn" due to the acid content of the fixer. Use the heat treatment at the lower temperature if you have more than one overprint.

DOILY (NAPKIN) III—HALF OVERPRINT

Use modular blocks A and K. Block A is the background block without pattern, while a parallelogram has been cut into block K (see top drawing opposite). This is a negative "harlequin figure" —a hole in the block.

We used one color in two shades, for example, a green mixed from blue and yellow, with the background green lightened with extender. We used a darker shade for the overprint. Always use a darker color than the background for overprinting because of the transparency of the colors.

When the background is dry, overprint with the pattern block, block K. On the upper row, overprint on the left half of each background print. On the second row overprint the right half of the squares. Continue alternating in this manner.

DOILY (NAPKIN) IV—REPEAT PRINTING

The repeat print plays a large role in fabric printing. We have mentioned it several times before. Repeat printing means that a regularly repeated block pattern is used and the repetition creates a larger and continuous pattern. You can cut the repeat block so the pattern can be made continuous both horizontally and vertically. In this case you can cover an entire surface with the pattern. If the repeat pattern is continuous in only one direction it makes a good border or linear pattern.

See the motif shown that we call the lesser part of the pattern. Four crooked angles form a kind of cross in the negative (see positive and negative prints, page 37). On the photograph of doily IV on page 41 you can see how the negative crosses form vertical and horizontal lines while at the same time four-pointed stars appear when you repeat this pattern (see page 43, bottom). First print the negative square (lower illustration) and then overprint with the negative cross pattern above.

Drawing the repeats: A so-called "true" repeat must fit horizontally and vertically. When sketching a repeat it's best to start off with a diagonal cross, a center cross (with a vertical and horizontal axis), or diameters in a circle. These three possibilities are shown in the diagrams on page 44. Here you can see how different stars, four-pointed and eight-pointed, can be laid out.

Draw the repeat for the doily over a cross.

The drawing for a repeat pattern and the cutting must be

extremely accurate. If the negative cross on the block is not very precise, for example, the effect of the line is lost.

Printing the doily (napkin): The background prints that have been used up to now do not have patterns cut in them. In this case we are going to use a background block in which we have cut a negative square. We left enough area on the block to give the doily a background color. Both blocks used for this doily are A blocks. We used two grey colors, with the lightest as background.

Breadbasket napkins—printing slightly larger projects

Using the same principles as in making the doilies, you can now go on to making a whole series of items in somewhat larger sizes. You can print them in the same colors and patterns to make sets.

BREADBASKET NAPKIN I

In the photographs on pages 45 and 46 we show two napkins. The procedure is the same as for other types of napkins. You can vary the measurements and the patterns, so you won't be merely making copies of our designs.

The first napkin is in one color. To obtain the darker shade on the sides in the pattern borders, we have simply used overprinting. It could be done in two colors instead.

Since this napkin is not square, like the doilies, the printing is done in another procedure:

The finished napkin measures $8\frac{1}{4}$ in. $\times$ $12\frac{1}{2}$ in. This size corresponds to 6×9 squares printed with modular block A, which measures $1\frac{3}{8}$ in. $\times$ $1\frac{3}{8}$ in. Of course, you may design your own modular system and vary the sizes. You may vary the design here by using another size modular block or by making a larger or smaller number of squares.

The blocks: We used two A blocks. One has a pattern and one does not. Both must be flocked.

The patterned block is easy to cut since the pattern consists only of a diagonal line. The drawing on page 45 shows how to cut this diagonal. One side of the line follows the diagonal of the block while the other is offset $\frac{3}{16}$ in. to $\frac{1}{4}$ in. In this way you will obtain a diagonal of white canals in the print. The cut lines must be parallel and exactly straight. When printed together a repeat print emerges as a zigzag line. You can also use this block for a center pattern where four prints together would make a square or cross, depending on how you point the block. (Do remember to glue an imprint design on the back of the block so you can see what you're doing.)

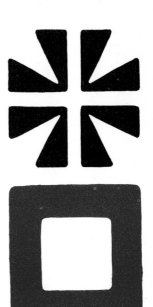

Basic Principles

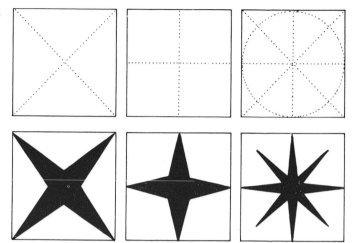

Sketch repeats on a simple idea, such as a diagonal, cross, and circle.

Outline and background printing: Fold the material as for the doilies —edge to edge to make a vertical and horizontal fold, indicating the axis of the length and width of the material.

Stretch out the material along the grain on the printing table, using straight pins or tape. If you use pins, insert them at an angle into the material and far enough out so the points do not get in the printing area.

Since there are an *odd* number of prints (nine) in the length of the napkin, position the first two prints in the middle row one on either side of the lengthwise axis, and with an equal amount of the pattern block above and below the crosswise axis. Whether the block is square or rectangular you must position it this way if your rows are an uneven number.

It is important to mark the block clearly so you show the exact center of each side of the block. Mark this with a pencil line on the top of the block so you can see it when you work (see page 71).

After you have made the two first prints, continue with two prints on the right side, then two prints on the left side.

Now print the row below. Print from left to right and continue this way until you have done the two rows under the first middle row. After this, print the pattern border with the cut-out block, which you must turn between each imprint if you want to make the zigzag pattern. Then print the last row of the background printing. (Overprinting the pattern border is done after the print is dry.) Turn the project and make the background prints in the same manner on the other half of the material plus the border. It is a bit difficult to turn the project if the napkin is pinned to the printing

44

table, so you could print away from yourself on the other half of material. If you're printing larger jobs, such as table runners and the small tablecloths, you must take out the pins and turn the material. Remember, you do get the best print when you print toward yourself. Finally, overprint the two borders precisely and make sure the block is turned in the right direction.

BREADBASKET NAPKIN II
This napkin is somewhat larger than the first one. The background has rows of 7 squares × 10 squares and uses modular block A (1¾ in. × 1¾ in.). The final size is 9⅝ in. × 13¾ in. Add hem allowance to this.

The materials are the same as for napkin I. In addition to block A, we use rectangular block B (1¾ in. × 2¾ in.) for the inside pattern. Block B has twice the surface of block A.
The blocks: Both block A, used for the background print, and block B, with the cut pattern, must be flocked.

The pattern is a kind of extension of the diagonal pattern used on the previous napkin. Notice how the angle in the repeat print creates squares of four white lines. The dark triangles in the corners become squares in the repeat print, and the white triangles form hourglass-shaped figures inside the repeat print. This geometrical pattern, consisting exclusively of straight lines, is easy to draw and cut. The block on page 47 is shown in full size.

To assure straight lines in drawing and cutting, and so avoid

---

Materials
White poplin or muslin, approx. 9 in. × 13 in.
Blocks: two modular blocks A.
Color: Own choice such as blue, green, 3.5 oz.
Miscellaneous: usual tools and materials for printing—printing table or printing board, inking pad with cloth (one cloth for each color), brush, straight pins, tape, stylus, trial cloth, etc.

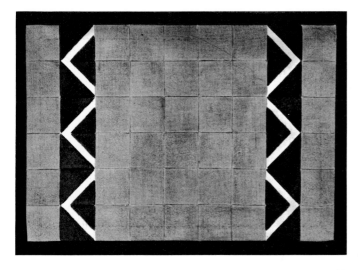

An easy breadbasket napkin with a single border pattern.

Basic Principles

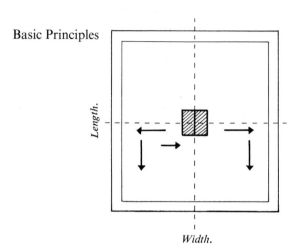

Length.

Width.

risk of spoiling the block, check and measure with a piece of graph paper before cutting.

Mark your printing block at the middle of each side.

Arrangement and printing of the center pattern: Fold the material in the usual manner to make the center cross for positioning. The center pattern consists of three rows of three prints. In this case,

Another breadbasket napkin with a geometrical motif in the center. There are many ways to vary the layout of designs on small projects. We did not print the pattern very *precisely, in order to show what a beginner's work might look like. Accuracy comes with skill and practice.*

46

where you have an odd number of prints on each side, the first print must be positioned exactly in the middle of the cross. Use the lines you have made on your block to position your first print exactly in the center. After the first print, position another print on each side. Then make three prints under this first row and three prints above the first row.

(If you had used an A block, you would have had to position the first print on top of the longitudinal fold, lined up along one side of the cross fold.)

After doing the center design, print the border that surrounds the pattern.

Making the background printed border: We used only one color for this napkin, too. As before, make the dark shade by over-printing.

Start printing in the middle of one of the long sides at the fold and work out toward the sides up to the corners. Then print along one of the short sides, again working from the middle out up to the corners. Continue in this way all around. Print the corners last.

Print the outer border the same way.

Finally, overprint the outer border row to create the dark border.

ARRANGEMENTS OF SIMILAR PROJECTS

If there are an even number of prints in the vertical direction, but an odd number in the width, place the first print right under the horizontal center line, covering the vertical center line (diagram 1).

If there are an even number of prints in both directions, for projects larger than doilies but smaller than tablecloths (see

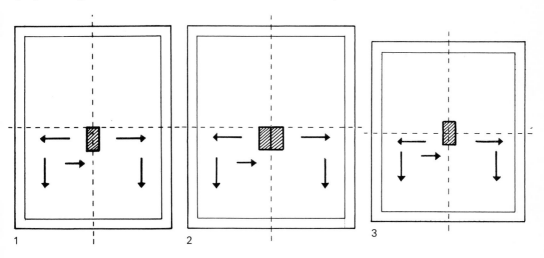

1   2   3

Basic Principles   page 71), place the first print under the horizontal fold and on both sides of the vertical fold (diagram 2).

For an odd number of prints in both directions, use the procedure shown in diagram 3.

You can print the doilies and napkins in many different ways. You can also do small table runners. The sketches below show six suggestions for arranging patterns and background blocks. The hatching indicates the background printing and the white spaces with lines sketched in indicate the patterns. The pattern is only suggested; the rest is up to you.

VARIATIONS

You can use the block for napkin II to print a border such as is done in napkin I, or you can print a border along both short and long sides. You can also print vertical stripes along the napkin with background prints in between. You could cover the entire napkin with pattern prints and have a border of background prints.

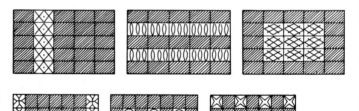

Here are several variations in schematic form for positioning the patterns. Even with the same pattern blocks, you can obtain quite different results by varied positioning and color effects.

48

PROJECTS

Background printing with cork blocks

You can make prints with many different kinds of materials if you apply paint to them. You can use a piece of wood and make a print of the grain structure, or you can use a leaf, a piece of corrugated cardboard, and the like. Such prints will reproduce their own structure lines.

You can do many enjoyable things with these objects, but you must realize that this kind of printing tends to look cheap and unartistic. Actually you need a very good eye for design in order to exploit the structure of materials in an artistic way.

There is one kind of structural printing that is suitable and fun to use. That is the cork print. This printing technique is suitable for background printing, such as for an apron as described on page 51.

Use the same printing method as for linoleum blocks, that is, the inking pad. But it is not necessary to flock or lacquer the cork.

You can get cork at art supply shops. Buy cork in 9 in. $\times$ 12 in. pieces and cut them into blocks with side ratio of 1 : 2 so you can use them together for overprinting when you want to make squares. Several thicknesses of cork are available: $\frac{1}{16}$ in., $\frac{1}{8}$ in., and $\frac{1}{4}$ in.

Besides this, you can buy a sanding block of cork. And in shops that sell sailing gear, you can buy larger pieces of cork to cut into suitable sizes. This kind of cork is very coarse, however.

When you buy cork for printing you must make sure the surface is reasonably even and that the corners of the sheets have right angles. Ask to see the selection and choose the best.

If the surface is not even, sand it on sandpaper just as you did with the linoleum block (see page 22). If you have a piece without right angles, you'll need to use a saw to make true right angles. Otherwise you'll get uneven lines between the prints when you do background printing.

You can get cork with either very open or with rather closed

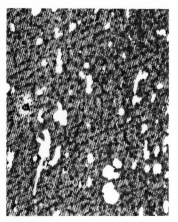

Imprint of cork reproduced to size. You can get a feel for the heavy structured effect of cork.

surfaces. Both types can be used. The open cork gives a "spotted" print that often requires an overprint with the block turned in the opposite direction if there is too much space between "spots." You can overprint with another color, as on the block photographed. Prints of this type may also serve as color experiments in an attempt to achieve color harmonies.

If the cork is too coarse, fill the holes with plastic wood, available in small cans at hardware and paint stores. Use a putty knife or wall scraper to spread the filler in the holes. When the plastic wood has dried, sand it smooth. Plastic wood that has dried out in the can may be restored by adding acetone, if it is not too old.

A hole that is too large in the cork may be used as decoration in a print, but as a rule it will have to be balanced by other holes cut in the block.

The tighter cork makes interesting overall prints due to the many small surface pores. Background printing with this type of cork can be done in a single color, or may be done in alternating colors, with or without overprinting.

It is possible to cut patterns in cork, but in this case you must choose a rather coarse pattern since the material does not permit fine cutting details. Cut with a very sharp pocket knife. You cannot use a cutter set for this job. The knife cuts more easily through the cork if you moisten the blade with water.

You can overprint a cork background with a linoleum block print. In this case the pattern and background prints must suit each other so the coarse background effect will harmonize with the block design.

Clean the cork with water, soap, and a brush after using. The cork block must be completely dry before you use it again.

Basic skirt and apron pattern

BACKGROUND PRINT WITH PATTERN BORDER
You can use the same printing technique for an apron as for the breadbasket napkin. The apron in the picture on page 52 is very simple to make. Start off with a rectangular piece of material and just use a background print with a space left for the border.

PROCEDURE
The pattern layout for the apron is shown on the diagram on page 53. Don't cut the different sections of material apart but stretch the whole piece of fabric out along the grain on the printing table as usual, using pins or tape, working from left to right. If the

50

material is larger than the printing board, roll the excess and cover it with tissue paper or newspaper.

Mark a line $\frac{3}{16}$ in. in from the top and the left edges of the fabric. Use a pencil to make the lines, which will be hidden in the hem.

The two marked lines will serve as a guide for the printing blocks.

Mark the vertical lines separating the apron strings and the waistband from the main section of the apron by a fold line, or mark with a stylus. You will be printing over these two lines. The material for the waistband needs to be printed twice to get the darker print.

In this case, don't start with a cross in the center fold, since this method works only for small projects. Instead, use the more professional technique of starting in the upper left-hand corner and printing horizontal rows, literally one after the other.

Check to see that the first row is accurately lined up with your marking lines. If the print "dips" correct the mistake as shown on page 38. When you print the next row (and following rows) position prints exactly in relation to the previous prints and the vertical line mark along the left side.

If you have marked a square grid on the fabric of your printing

Background printing with cork. We printed the material at the left with open cork and overprinted with the same piece of cork in another color. The colors are yellow and green. We turned the cork block around in order to avoid having the second print exactly on top of the first print.

To the right cork background print with an overprint in linoleum block. The background is red and overprint is black. The chessboard pattern appears whenever you print every other background block twice.

When you print with cork, the background print will have a special character only obtained by using cork. Don't spoil this effect by letting the overprint cover too much of the background.

Use cork prints sparingly. It is a chancy technique. Textile printing ought to be a "deliberate creation."

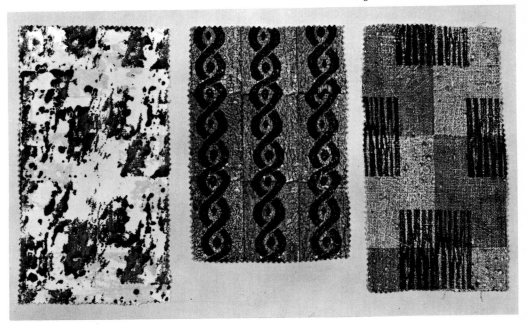

Projects   table, you will already have the necessary guide lines for precise prints right on hand. If you lack this grid, use graph paper instead. You can mark off the size of the block on this. Check with the graph paper on both sides of the print for each row you print. You could also use ordinary paper on which you have marked off the size of the block you are using.

This apron is done with the lower rows overprinted in the same color.

When you get to the pattern border, print this immediately since the block has the same measurements as the background block, so you can use the prints in the previous row as your guide. If you are going to print the border with a spaced pattern (see page 68) calculate the width of the border area. Draw the outer edge with a stylus along a ruler—if a stylus is not available use a very light pencil line—and print the last row of background prints. (Don't

Materials
Muslin, poplin, or fine linen, 19¾ in. × 31½ in.
Blocks: Modular block H. Use two, one with pattern and one without, but both possibly flocked.
Color: Light green.

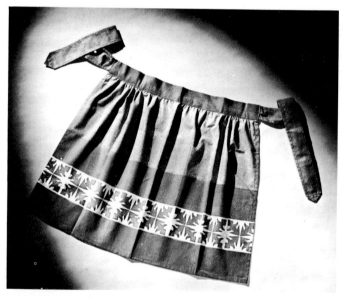

Apron printed with a large block. The motif in the border is symmetrical and constructed on two diagonals. We created the pattern on the basis of a paper-cut design. The paper-cut is made in the same size as the block so it is easy to transfer the motif.

52

mark the border before getting to it because the background prints may possibly shift a little along the way.) Then finally print the pattern with the patterned block.

By the way, only print the pattern on the part of the material that makes up the apron proper—not on the waistband and strings.

If there is not room for a whole block print on the pattern, cover the material with paper so the overlap part of the pattern won't print on the fabric.

For the border motif you could also use a completely different block in the same width as the background block ($2\frac{3}{4}$ in.) A block $1\frac{3}{8}$ in. wide would also work, since it is easy to position and is half of a background print.

You might want to mark the position of the prints in advance with straight pins stuck down into the already printed material so that you don't print over them.

If you prefer, you can vary the project by initially covering the material with a background print. When this is dry, make the pattern as an overprint on one or more rows using a color darker than the background prints.

You can make a skirt in the same way as the apron.

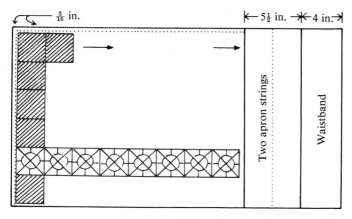

Pattern diagram for apron. The same principle is used for skirts. Print from the top downwards in horizontal rows. The vertical row to the left shows how you can make room for the pattern border, if you don't print it when you do the background print. See text.

53

Aprons—following a paper diagram

The pattern is made up of background printing and masking. The apron shown in the photograph differs from the previous one in shape and printing technique. The print is a brick pattern achieved by background printing with overprinting, masked along a curve all the way around to provide space for a border.

The outer edge of the pattern with the curved shape was obtained by the masking technique that consists of printing part of the background block on a paper mask pre-cut to the desired shape.

This printing technique is also used for the overblouse described on page 89.

PATTERN DIAGRAM

Cut out the diagram pattern on absorbent wrapping paper as shown in the drawing (page 56). Draw the circle with a pencil and string (see page 85). As you can see on the drawing you have to "flatten out" the circle a bit by eye.

When you have cut the material, cut away the outer round strip of the paper pattern. This strip will be used to cover the border area when you print the background area.

Now stretch the fabric along the grain on the printing table and fasten with pins or tape. Place the cut paper strip over the outer edge of the material. Tack the strip with tape or pins; place pins only in places you are not going to print.

PRINTING

Background print: Start printing with the background block D and the light color, since as a rule you always start printing with the lightest color. Print out from the "X" on the diagram to each side. The prints must accurately follow the upper edge of the fabric. You could draw a line along this edge, as you did with the previous apron. This would serve as a guide for printing. This can be done with pencil, since it will later be hidden by the waistband.

When you get out to the sides, let the last print overlap the masking paper. Print the next row exactly under the first row, working from left to right.

When you have covered the material completely with background prints, place the cut-out pocket on the printed fabric, exactly where it will later be sewn on, and mark the positions of the block prints with very light pencil lines or a stylus. Now you can place the pocket on a piece of paper and print it so the designs will

line up accurately. The background print on the pocket will completely match the apron pattern.

Overprinting: The overprint forms the background pattern. The diagram on page 58 shows how the pattern emerges. Use modular block C for the printing and the same color that was used for the background printing. Mark the middle of the block with a clearly visible line, for shifting the design.

Print the first print in the upper left half of the first background print. As you continue, position the prints on the left side of every other section (number 1 on the diagram).

Next print in the upper right half of the blocks in between those you printed first. (Second block in top row of diagram on page 58.) Cover the fabric with paper, as explained earlier, to catch the part that extends beyond the design area. Use the middle mark on your block as a guide.

Now print in the lower right half of the first section (first block in top row of diagram) and halfway down into the next row (number 2 in diagram), and continue in the alternate blocks in this manner.

Print again in the second row in the left sides of every other section, but this time it is offset one block from the first row (number 3

Rounded apron with a pattern in the background print. Use the same color for background and overprint. We used cork blocks in module sizes, but linoleum blocks are excellent, too.

55

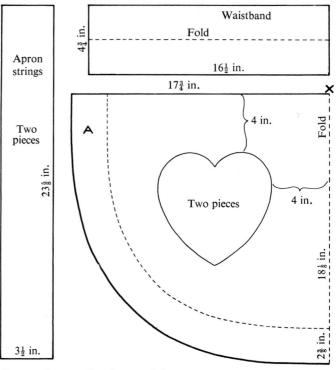

Materials
Poplin, muslin, or fine linen, 17¾ in. × 35½ in.

Blocks: Modular blocks D and C and triangular modular block R3 (49.5 × 49.5 × 60 mm.)

Colors: 3.5 oz. light yellow for background and 1.75 oz. dark yellow for triangular border.

Apron strings

Two pieces

23⅝ in.

3½ in.

Waistband

Fold

4¾ in.

16½ in.

17¾ in.

Fold

4 in.

Two pieces

4 in.

18⅛ in.

2⅜ in.

A

Pattern diagram for the rounded apron.

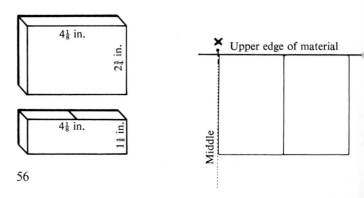

4⅛ in.

2¾ in.

4⅛ in.

1⅜ in.

✕ Upper edge of material

Middle

56

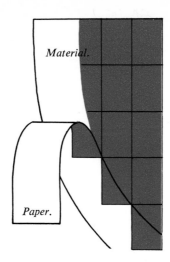

Material.

Paper.

Print out over the paper mask that covers the border. Be careful not to print on the printing-table cloth— that would make the cushion stiff and uncomfortable to work on.

on the diagram). In this way a step-like pattern emerges. When you come to the edge, part of the print will go on the masking paper.

When you have finished overprinting, place the pocket on the material again and mark the positions for the overprinting. Lay the pocket on a piece of paper and overprint it.

Print the waistband and apron strings by themselves using a background block, without overprinting. For the apron in the photograph we used a light color. Use masking paper underneath, so printing that extends beyond the width of the material you want will not print on the printing table (see drawing above). Print the lining of the pocket once, using the background block and a light color.

The border: Finally, print the border around the apron. Use a triangular background block for this.

Cover the center area of the apron with the paper pattern piece, so the only material that remains uncovered is the border area. Your printed material will be covered and protected by the paper. In this way you won't get undesired printing on the work you have already done.

Now start—and this is an exception—with the dark color. These will be the triangles that are adjacent to the apron's main area. Print over the mask so the base line of the triangle gets a gentle curve and you avoid white space between the areas.

Finally print in the light triangles in the remaining spaces at the outside of the border. Clean the block before you change color.

Projects

The diagram shows the overprint
sequence. First print everything
marked 1, then everything marked 2,
then 3, and so on.

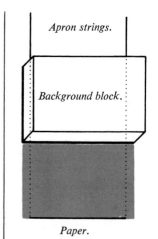

Apron strings.

Background block.

Paper.

Place the apron strings on the paper
and print out over the edge with the
background block.

Patterns in background print have many possibilities for variation, as on this apron. We made the large pocket by simply folding the lower part of the fabric double. We printed the pocket with a block with stylized flowers and used the same principle as for the apron on page 55.

ORIGINAL BACKGROUND PATTERNS

Using the procedures described, you can make your own patterns. Cut out pieces of paper the size of the C block. Experiment by placing these pieces on your background print in different arrangements. Let the paper pieces stay in place when you have a design you like. Don't remove them until you are ready to print, so you won't get the pattern wrong.

The stylized flower pattern on the pocket for the larger apron.

Borders and corners

RHYTHM AND MELODY

Borders and corners are essential elements in textile printing projects such as a tablecloth and the like. A border usually will be a rhythmic repetition on one or more pattern elements, motifs following each other in a definite system.

Geometric border containing several pattern elements. When you repeat this print the rhythm emerges by itself. A border like this does create corner problems.

59

The drawings on these two pages are intended only as sketches, not as textile print borders. You may deduce from the drawings that borders may be divided into two groups: those that are continuous and those that consist of loose single units that clearly mark the print of each block. The continuous patterns give the tightest impression and lead your eyes around the border.

The simplest rhythm may look like this:

Like playing on a keyboard using only one key with the same interval.

Now, add a new note.

And here play a more varied melody.

You can vary this melody in many ways.

The same pattern elements reappear but the distribution is no longer a 1–2 beat.

Where opposites meet, a melody emerges in addition to the beat.

Not only the figures determine the music. Changing colors gives more voices.

The interplay between shapes and lines is important for the border, as here between vertical and horizontal.

The border may be closed.

Or it may be open.

It can be spread out.

60

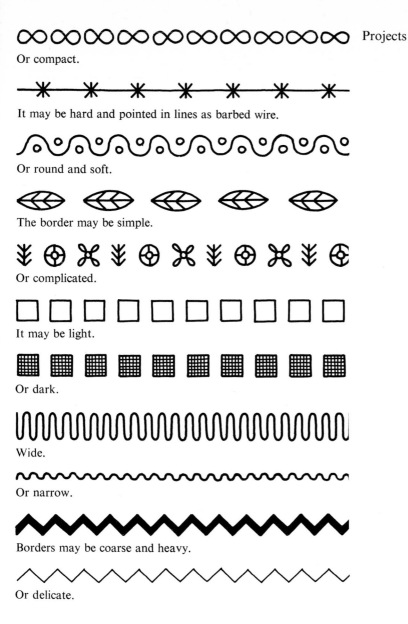

Or compact.

It may be hard and pointed in lines as barbed wire.

Or round and soft.

The border may be simple.

Or complicated.

It may be light.

Or dark.

Wide.

Or narrow.

Borders may be coarse and heavy.

Or delicate.

There are many possibilities. Here are only a few that suggest how large a register you may play upon. The appearance of the border depends on what it is going to frame, or whether it is going to

61

At the top, easy borders without problems. Below, a border motif for a child's outfit. The pattern is printed in repeat so that the elephants hold each other's tails as in the circus. Notice the corner.

Make the corners in the upper border as shown by means of a special corner block that repeats the theme of the pattern. The lower border also has a different corner. However, the pattern resembles the border. The same is true of the border shown in the photograph.

62

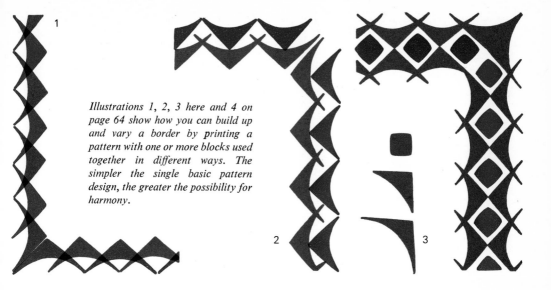

Illustrations 1, 2, 3 here and 4 on page 64 show how you can build up and vary a border by printing a pattern with one or more blocks used together in different ways. The simpler the single basic pattern design, the greater the possibility for harmony.

1

2

3

stand alone as decoration. It may be neutral boundary for a pattern or a continuation of the theme of the pattern. (Geometrical borders are by far the easiest to work with.)

PROBLEMS WITH CORNERS AND BORDERS

Borders will present difficulties especially when you are about to turn the corner. You must strive to make the turns an integral part of the border. Solve each corner problem individually, but you may find several equally suitable alternatives. Below are some possible solutions.

Borders without problems: The example top right (page 62) shows a simple border printed with two square blocks. One has a square cut out in the middle and the other has no pattern. In this case the corner forms by itself as if you used only the background print blocks.

The border of hearts uses the same motif in the corners, but the corner heart is turned so the bend looks natural.

Borders with contrasting corners: As in one of the examples you can print a corner with a block pattern that is not the border motif, but fits well with the border pattern. For the border shown in the picture we used the form elements of the border to make the contrasting corner print.

On the drawing of the stylized flower border the corner motif is not a duplicate of the other flowers, but is similar in character.

Projects

4

Borders made up of several block prints: The examples on page 63 are all related since they are composed of the same form elements— curved angles. For the first border we used only one angle with two colors printed overlapping each other. The corner appears where right sides of the angles meet. In the next example we used a large and small angle. The points of the large ones cross over each other in the print. The corner is formed without overlapping. At this corner the angles don't meet. The third border is somewhat more complicated. Here we only used the large angles point against point to make a wider border. We printed a rectangle with slightly curved sides inside the resulting rectangular holes. In this way the corner literally takes care of itself. In the fourth border, pictured above, we show how both angles may be used for a wider border —printing the smaller angles against each other inside, forming an oval between them, while outside the large angles close off the border motif.

Two geometrical borders. You can turn each of these to make a corner.

Overprint borders: We used a block cut out as an irregular pentagon for a border. In the overprinting, done in a contrasting color, we turned the block. The result is a "harlequin figure" in rectangles with broken corners. Only through sketching and playing with the linoleum blocks can you get this type of pattern, which is not easy to visualize in your imagination.

The basic element in the next border is a pyramid figure which is slightly overprinted on top of the first print.

The mirror method: To visualize how a corner block will look, use a pocket mirror as an aid. The photograph opposite shows how to do this. Hold the mirror at an angle of 45 degrees on the border.

64

When you hold a mirror at the top of the border at a 45-degree angle, you can get an idea how the corner will look when you turn the border. Then you can decide how to treat this corner. Pre-plan the corner treatment before you get to it, or you may have an unpleasant surprise. You can make minor adjustments by pulling or pushing the fabric a little to get the corners to fit. But it is better to calculate in advance.

When you then look in the mirror you will see how the border appears in a right angle and how you should then draw the corner motif.

The method is easy and excellent.

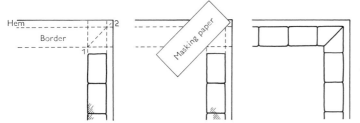

How to print a correct border corner. Mark the center line for the corner 1–2 and cover half of the corner with paper on which the rest of the imprint will print. Then do the other half the same way.

Covering corners: You will often need this type of corner construction especially when you print the border with a background block.

The principle is the same as joining corners of a picture frame. The print will simply be cut off diagonally when you cover the corner with a piece of masking paper. On the diagram, above, the cut is indicated by the diagonal broken line and the numbers 1 and 2. Place the masking paper all the way out to the corner of the material so the cutting line is not crooked. When you remove the mask after printing, you have half of the corner. Place the mask on the other side in the opposite position, and print the other half of the corner.

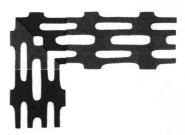

Diagonal cutting of a corner.

65

If you use a modular block, for the border, that corresponds to the background or pattern print, it is easy to place the prints so they fit along the central prints. Print around as shown by the arrows. In spaced design borders, start to print in the middle and print toward the sides. Mark the exact position for the prints with straight pins.

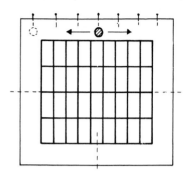

Instead of merely making an edge, border patterns are good for decorating belts, narrow wall hangings, or for stripes on a tablecloth or curtain.

How to make spaced design borders. Make several prints of the block on paper or pieces of fabric and cut them out. Place them on the fabric you are to print. After they are in position put a straight pin along the side of the fabric indicating the center of each design block. If you have a long ruler you can make sure the lines are equidistant. Or you might use the background block as a guide if it fits in between.

With the mirror method you can see if a border pattern is suitable for this corner treatment. The overprinted borders on page 64 can be treated in this way. The border of squares and "harlequin figures" must be turned over the diagonal of one of the squares (check it yourself with a mirror). The border on page 65 can be cut off diagonally in the corner with the masking method. In this case we are dealing with a smaller repeat (the repeat itself is indicated with color).

LAYING OUT BORDERS

When you lay out a border it is best to use graph paper to sketch on. The modular system is also helpful here.

Plan the border, using the graph squares, by choosing a basic block size. The A block might correspond to one square, the B block to two squares, and the C block to three squares on your

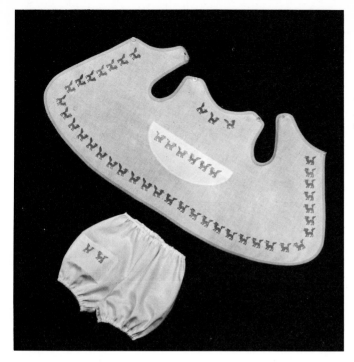

Child's outfit with a printed cat border. Note that we cut two blocks but that one is reversed so that the cats will face each other in the center of the border. This kind of border has no corner problems. Use delicate patterns for babies or small children. You can easily copy this pattern from the photograph.

graph paper. Use graph paper both for borders done in a row and for those that are spaced out.

The graph paper is especially helpful when you are using a patterned block for corners that can be cut off diagonally at only one

Border designs cut with scissors, here in an old traditional Polish motif.

67

place. If you pre-plan, you won't be unpleasantly surprised by impractical results.

USES FOR BORDERS

In each case you must decide which border will be best suited for a specific use. Usually a heavily-patterned project will be held together best by a background printed border, while a calm background-printed center section could take a more lively border.

The pattern on this tablecloth is from Polish peasant paper-cuts. The patterns are printed with blocks that do not fit the modular system. This does not make a problem because you can print them free in the border area. The corner block is not symmetrical, but the effect is still good. Because of the distortion in the photograph the background prints appear square, but they are not. See text, page 70.

68

If you want to work with patterns of this type, flowers and imaginary animals, you can find them on old woodcuts in peasant art collections. You can also make rubbings of them. Place a piece of paper on top and rub over the paper with a grease pencil the same way you do when you make rubbings with the flat end of a wooden pencil.

The bird design printed on these doilies was copied from a woodcut in a mangling board in the Danish National Museum. You could use this design for a tablecloth border. If you are printing doilies, be sure to use the leftover colors before they dry out.

The border width must also be compatible with the size of the pattern to make an overall harmonic appearance. Too delicate a frame around a heavy center section, or too bold a border around a light center, will spoil the overall impression. This is true not only for the width of the border but also for its design. Similar considerations should go into the corner treatment.

Tablecloths, pillow cases, and curtains

From smaller textile printing projects we now proceed to the larger items. The technique is the same except for a change in the sequence of positioning the printing.

First try the pattern and colors on a small object such as a napkin for a breadbasket to get the general effect. It will be wise to remember that small projects require patterns that are not too large and bold and that large projects often require larger pattern units.

ARRANGEMENT

Figuring out the pattern arrangement has been rather easy up to

Start to print at one of the short sides. Start from the center axis and print out to the sides. If there are an even number of prints in the width, place the first print on each side of the center fold. With an odd number of prints, place the first print on the center fold.

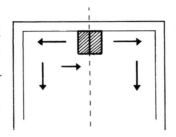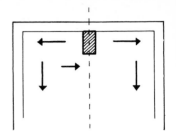

now. More figuring is required for a tablecloth, but it is easy enough if you first sketch out the arrangement on graph paper.

One graph square can equal a block print.

As previously done, start from a center cross marking the axis of the length and width of the material. Use the cross to measure by simply counting the number of squares vertically and horizontally, both for background and pattern print.

Then multiply the number of vertical squares by the measurement of the side of the block and this gives you the extent of the pattern in that direction. Add to this hem allowance and possibly extra material for a white border if desired. Do the same for the horizontal side.

As mentioned, let one square equal one block print. Or you could use the modular system and let the A block equal one square and the B block equal three squares, etc.

When you cut the material don't figure the size too closely. If despite all the care you exercise, you have figured half an inch or so wrong, you can save the project if there is a little extra material all the way around.

POLISH-INSPIRED TABLECLOTH PRINTED ON COLORED FABRIC

The tablecloth pictured on page 68 is printed on yellow sateen. When printing on colored materials, you must realize that the print colors change shade because of their transparency. Always use a color that is darker than the color of the material. For the tablecloth we used a brown print color.

Before you start printing on colored material, make a test print on a left-over piece of material. Glue or tack the test print in a notebook with all the necessary information on the kind of fabric and textile color mixtures used.

Materials in pastel colors are best suited for printing. You can print on darker materials if you use opaque colors, which are

Materials for tablecloth
Yellow satin, 40 in. × 70 in. or a size suitable for your needs.

Blocks: modular block D for background print. Border block ($3\frac{3}{4}$ in. × $5\frac{1}{2}$ in.—not a modular block), corner block ($3\frac{1}{2}$ in. × $3\frac{1}{2}$ in.—not a modular block).

Color: Brown, approximately $5\frac{3}{4}$ oz.

Miscellaneous: Additional materials and tools for textile prints as listed earlier. For indicated measurement, the background block will print 8 times in the width and 10 times in the length.

70

available in stores, or very dark transparent colors. When using opaque colors you can also print with light on dark.

The brown colors used here can be bought ready-mixed, but you can mix your own. To obtain brown shades with the basic colors, mix yellow, red, and black.

MEASURING AND PRINTING

When printing larger projects don't use the method of working from a center cross. We use a more professional method of printing from the top of one of the short sides and working down toward you. This way places the prints in rows under each other (see diagrams opposite).

Fold the material as usual to make a cross in the center. The area of the completed central background print is 22 in. × 41¼ in. when you use the block suggested here. Find the horizontal lines that limit the pattern by measuring 20⅝ in. in from the center cross along the long axis and similarly the vertical lines by measuring 11 in. to each side along the cross axis. Mark these lines clearly by folding or with a stylus.

During this procedure remember that there should be room for the open patterned border, which is 4⅜ in. wide, and the 2¼ in. wide solid color border outside that. Print this latter border with the background block, which is 2¾ in. wide. Remember that the borders (as always) are printed last. Stretch the material out along the grain on the printing table (smooth out the measuring folds). Roll the material that won't fit on the printing table and cover it with tissue paper. You may use straight pins in the sides to hold the roll together.

Since there are eight background prints across the width of the material, first make a print at the top on each side of the vertical center axis. Then continue out to the sides.

When you have printed the first row, print the row underneath and continue with the following rows, making sure the rows of prints are exact.

GRAPH PAPER

When you print large projects, such as this tablecloth, there is a certain risk that you might unknowingly and almost imperceptibly shift the printing so the entire pattern no longer has right-angled corners. Control this by using a piece of graph paper on which the length of the block is measured out 10 times, one after the other. Check each row with the graph paper, both at the right and left sides. If it turns out that a row has come out crooked, correct this gradually in the following rows.

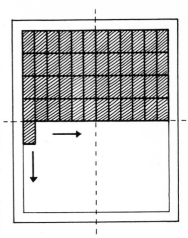

The background print should form a precise rectangle. You must continuously check by measuring constantly as you print. The sketch indicates the work sequence.

If the block doesn't fit the desired size of the tablecloth, you can cover the two outer rows to diminish the area of the prints. Both ends must look alike for good appearance.

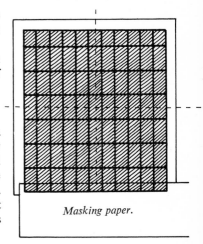

Masking paper.

Projects

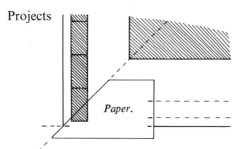 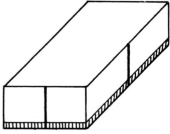

Paper.

For printing the corner of the Polish tablecloth the masking paper must follow the line between the corner of the background print and the corner of the material.

When printing over the center fold, it is important that the middle of the block is marked to insure an exact placement.

If you have marked a square grid on the cloth of the printing table, the precise positioning of the prints will be much easier (see page 28).

THE BORDER

The pattern in our tablecloth border was inspired by a Polish peasant motif. We used two patterns, a border pattern and a corner motif.

Print the border pattern first. Start off at the middle of one of the long sides and print out toward the end. Repeat the process for the other half. Space the prints evenly. Print the three other sides in the same way.

The border is $4\frac{3}{8}$ in. wide and since the block is only $3\frac{3}{4}$ in. wide you must place the prints exactly in the middle of the plain border area. As a guide, use a long piece of wooden molding or a ruler. Or mark the guide line with a stylus or clear tape. To arrange the pattern, follow the directions in the previous section (page 66).

Finally, print the corner motifs.

Now print the outer brown border with the background block used for the center. Cover the corners diagonally with a paper mask as described on page 65.

PLANNING

The planning is fun. Before you start, take some time to play with paper and pencil until you find out how to lay out the tablecloth. This technique, where background printing is combined with pattern printing, offers many possibilities. The sketch opposite shows some suggestions for printing tablecloths, but these are simply diagrammatic plans.

A corner motif for the Polish tablecloth.

72

PRINTING ON DYED MATERIAL

You could dye a piece of white material yourself, and then you could print on that. This could be done with a textile printing screen or in batik. As a rule, mentioned earlier, the color of the material must be lighter than the color of the prints, unless you use opaque colors.

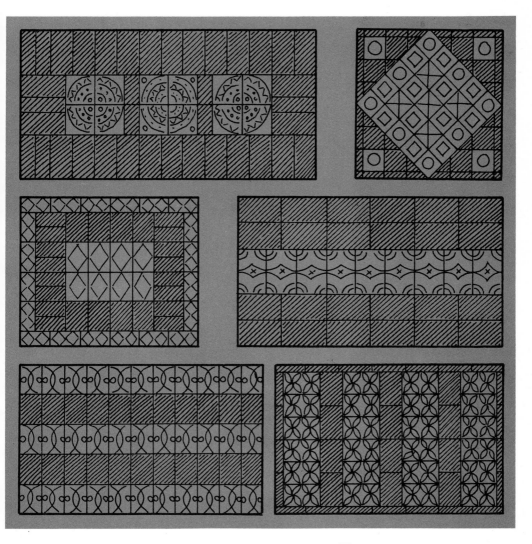

Projects OTHER TABLECLOTHS
Using the techniques we have described, you can make many table-cloth designs. On page 73 are several ideas for arranging the prints. The crosshatching indicates background blocks.

Tablecloths with patterned background printing

Using four different background blocks in modular sizes, we printed this tablecloth with light blue, dark *blue, and red, which created new colors in the overprinting.*

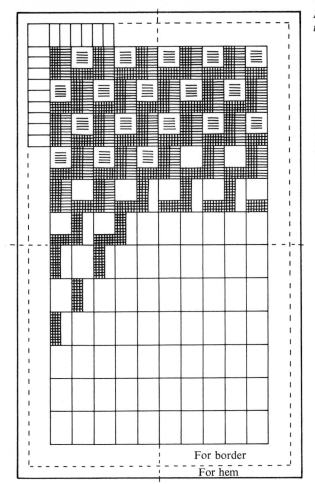

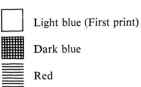

Here's a diagram for printing the tablecloth. See text for details.

☐ Light blue (First print)

▦ Dark blue

▤ Red

For border

For hem

BACKGROUND PATTERNS AND NEW COLORS BY OVERPRINTING

The tablecloth in the photograph is not so easy to print, but it is a good exercise in *printing precisely*. If you think the project is too large, start off by printing this or a similar background pattern on a smaller project. This tablecloth is intended for use on a narrow coffee table, but you can adapt the measurements to your own needs.

Because they can be combined like building blocks, the blocks of the modular system lend themselves to many experiments with background printing.

Materials
Linen or poplin 31½ in. × 73 in.
Blocks: A, B, C, and D and H for the corners. Possibly flock all blocks.
Colors: 1, light blue, 7 oz.; 2, dark blue, 3.5 oz.; 3, red, 2 oz.

75

Background printing with overprinting depends on the mutual relationship between the colored surfaces that make the pattern and color-play. Where the background is a patterned design, it is difficult and usually undesirable to add block prints with patterns.

PROCEDURE

The procedure for measuring and printing generally follows the one for the Polish-inspired tablecloth in the previous section.

First print: Use the D block which makes 12 prints in length by 10 prints in the width, not including the hem allowance and border. Print with the block's short side along the narrow sides of the material, using light-blue color.

Second print: Now we have the basis for the pattern. Print on top of the background print from the top and down, row after row. Start in the upper row at the left with the dark blue color and the C block, overprinting the left side of every other rectangle. Print the next row similarly but start with the second rectangle. In this way the prints alternate as you proceed downward.

Third print: Use B block and the dark blue color and make prints horizontally at the bottom in every other rectangle—the rectangles that haven't been overprinted (see diagram)—and shift them downward as before.

Fourth print: For this use the red color and the cleaned C block, which is half as wide as background block D. Make the prints next to the dark blue overprint (second print). Now all the background (first print) has been covered in every other rectangle.

Fifth print: Continue with the red color but now use the A block and make the prints in the remaining square light-blue areas. Place the prints exactly in the middle.

Printing the border: Use the light-blue color and the cleaned B block. Make the prints with the one short edge toward the pattern area (see diagram). The border consists of 36 prints in the length and 20 prints in the width. Fill in the squares at the corner with the H block, using the same color.

The colors: The color indications naturally must be considered only as our suggestions. If you want to use other combinations, experiment in advance to obtain colors that will match each other and harmonize with the overprint. When you overprint you risk getting a color that appears muddy—hence the need for experimenting.

Handbags and partial overprinting

You can print material for a handbag using a quite simple theme. Fold a rectangular piece of material in the usual way to make the center cross. The bottom of the bag will then be at the horizontal fold. You must consider this when planning and printing. If the bag is to have a top flap, the bottom will have to shift to correspond.

Each bag has its own measurements and shape. You can buy different handles or make braided straps for them.

In printing smaller bags start from the center cross and work out to the sides. Print larger bag as you would a tablecloth.

You can make handbags with background printing alone or with a combination of background printing and pattern blocks and a border running around the handbag. Stripes can be made using the long modular blocks. By overprinting in the other direction, the stripes become plaids. You can also print handbags on colored material (see page 70).

It would take too much space to explain the various finishing techniques used for handbags here, but the diagram on page 78 shows two ways to finish a dressy bag. You can also consult Grete Krønke's book *Mounting Handicraft* (Van Nostrand Reinhold).

PARTIAL OVERPRINTING

You can obtain a special effect in textile printing by shifting the print slightly. This is a double print, using the same blocks but with the print slightly shifted. You should not exaggerate this effect. Use

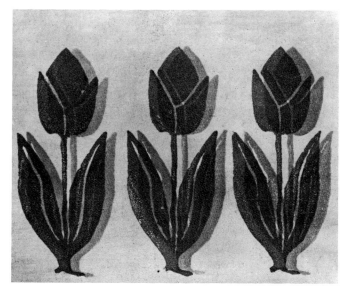

The shadow effect in the tulips comes from shifted prints or partial overprinting. They are printed on a piece of light-blue material with two blue-grey colors, a dark shade for the tulips and a lighter one for the shadow effect. Avoid violent contrasts with this printing method.

This original design is cut in an F block.

it with extreme caution. Always shift the print to the same side and the same amount. You can't use every block for this technique, so experiment first. In this technique it's only a small step from an elegant design, as shown, to what looks like a misprint!

The tulips in the illustration are very nicely suited to this kind of partial overprinting. Here the motif appears to be a shadow effect.

Depending on the size of the block, you can use this pattern as a motif for a handbag, a border for the bottom of a dress or apron, for an eyeglass case, pillow cover, etc.

For this handbag we used a 16 in. × 32 in. piece of material. Decide your size according to need. The middle of the material is marked M and will form the bottom. Drawing at right shows how to finish a bag with a ready-made handle from a craft shop.

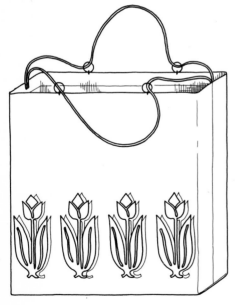

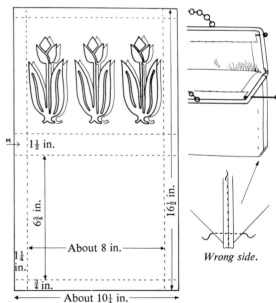

M → 1½ in.

6¾ in.

16½ in.

1¼ in.

About 8 in.

¾ in.

About 10¼ in.

Wrong side.

HELPFUL HINTS

If you cut incorrectly

Don't throw away a block if you've made a mistake on it. You can often salvage geometrical patterns so that you can use the block for some other project (see page 21). This goes for other blocks as well.

The following method is useful for large complicated patterns where it doesn't pay to start over again.

1. In this bird, copied from a Czech original in the Danish National Museum, the following mistakes were discovered: (*a*) the point of one of the wings came off; (*b*) the light areas in the middle of the

The repaired block. On left, notice the discarded piece from the body of the bird. A patch of this type will not show up in the finished print if you do a careful job.

bird were too large and looked like lakes; (*c*) the pilot-print edge wasn't cut completely clean.

2. Cut out an area around the faulty parts of the pattern. Cut in straight lines and all the way down to the wood. Take up the section without damaging the cut edges and clean off the strands of burlap and loose pieces of linoleum to make the wood stand out evenly and smoothly. Place the sections you cut out on a piece of linoleum and trace around the edge with a very sharp pencil as close to the edge of the section as possible. Cut out the pieces and fit them into the opening. Do not cut the pieces too small. Too large is better. Then you can sand them off with fine sandpaper until you get the proper fit. When the patch fits, glue it with water-fast hobby glue and put the block in a press for 48 hours (use a C clamp and a flat piece of wood to protect the linoleum surface). Now sand the patches with sandpaper to make them completely even. You can fill out any cracks with plastic wood and later smooth them with sandpaper.

3. After the patches have been glued in, cut out the correct pattern. At the same time cut the outer edge of the block clean to prevent any false prints.

4. Now the block is well repaired. Do not soak a patched block for very long in water when you clean it.

Folded paper-cuts

Folded paper designs are fun to make, but one can never be quite sure what will be the outcome. We are most familiar with the technique in making folded paper "snowflakes" or rows of stick figures.

The technique is simple. Take a square piece of paper and fold it three times to make a triangle. Fold it once again to make a smaller triangle. You might even want to fold it once more, depending on the size. A circle of paper can be folded this way, too.

80

Cut the design in straight or curved lines as shown. Use a paper square the same size as the block you will use for the print so you can transfer the design directly.

Tea cosy—printing with large blocks

The larger the block the more difficult it is to work with and get completely perfect prints. We call large blocks anything you can't reach around with your fingers.

It is important that the pattern cut is beveled on the large blocks so that delicate parts of the pattern won't be damaged from the hard pressure during printing (page 21).

Make a handle on the block. Use a suitable piece of wood screwed into the back of the block. Before mounting the handle, remember to glue a print of the block on the back of the block, even though the handle will cover part of it.

In order to get the color squeezed sufficiently down into the material when printing, use a cabinet-maker's mallet (as shown in the photograph on the next page) or a rubber mallet (also pictured).

Hammer evenly over the entire surface of the block, making sure the block doesn't shift position. Hold onto the handle while pounding.

The inking pad must be about $2\frac{1}{2}$ in. larger than the block.

TEA COSY

The motif for the tea cosy is pictured on page 83. If you don't have a knack for drawing, don't try these "drawn" motifs. Work, instead, with geometrical patterns. Freehand drawing will appear amateurish if you don't have a sure hand. Geometrical patterns present little risk (see "materials," next page).

Stretch out the two pieces of shantung next to each other to ensure that the prints will be positioned the same way on the front and on the back (see diagrams on page 83).

Use the lower 3 in. of the material to fold inside as a hem. Place the border above this fold line. As an exception, we start with the border here, since the pattern print consists of only one block.

Cut the B block with a border edge, as shown in the lower right drawing on page 83. Print the big block $\frac{3}{4}$ in. above the border.

You could fill out the fruits and tail feathers with a green color, using a technical pen, such as the Leroy lettering pen.

Tea cosy in miniature is an egg warmer. For such small projects use leftover paint.

FINISHING

Cut four pieces of material for the lining. Use unbleached muslin and cut it according to the diagram for the tea cosy (see page 83)

81

Trial printing a large block. Use a cabinet-maker's mallet or rubber mallet to make the print completely even. Pound the block down against the material. Use a stylus or make a soft fold for guide lines, instead of a ruler.

but make it 2 in. shorter. Sew these pieces together along the edge. Sew each set of lining pieces together. For an insert padding use cotton batting cut the same as the lining (or a thin sheet of foam). Place the stuffing between the lining pieces and fold the edges back toward each other at the bottom. Overcast the edges together.

Sew the printed fabric together along the edge (right sides together) and turn. Pull it over the finished insert lining. Fold the 3 in. hem inside and hem it to the lining.

The other two diagrams show tea cosies in varied shapes: a rectangle and a bishop's hat.

Printing in a circle

It's often pleasing to use a circular design on doilies (napkins), clothing, pillows, and the like. This method is used for the blouse on page 89.

CONSTRUCTING AND DIVIDING THE CIRCLE

When first making the layout for circular pattern it is helpful to use polar graph paper. For the arrangement and printing, it's practical to work with cut-out paper circles since they can be used both as a guide for the printing blocks and as a graph, and also as a mask.

A thin piece of brown paper will make a good pattern, but use

Materials

Heavy, natural-colored shantung, two pieces about 16½ in. × 15¾ in. In addition, four pieces of unbleached muslin in the same size. Use cotton batting for stuffing.

Blocks: Large block (not modular) 6 in. × 8¼ in. plus modular block B for border. Color: Approximately 2 oz. (a large inking cloth sucks up a lot of paint).

82

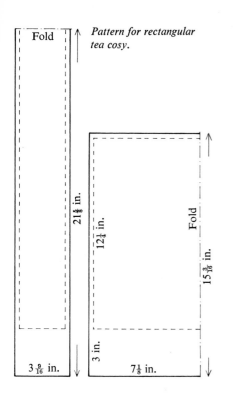

Pattern for rectangular tea cosy.

Fold

$21\frac{5}{8}$ in.

$3\frac{9}{16}$ in.

$12\frac{1}{4}$ in.

Fold

$15\frac{3}{16}$ in.

3 in.

$7\frac{1}{8}$ in.

Pattern for tea cosy and inside liner.

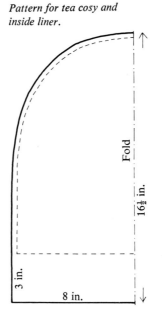

Fold

$16\frac{1}{2}$ in.

3 in.

8 in.

Pattern for mitered tea cosy.

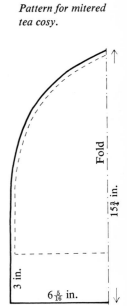

Fold

$15\frac{3}{4}$ in.

3 in.

$6\frac{5}{16}$ in.

Tea cosy printed with large blocks.

Border for tea cosy. Line makes a continuous border. The design repeat is made of one complete figure and two half-figures on a B block.

83

only smooth paper that has not been creased or previously used for wrapping.

If the circles are too large to be drawn with a compass, use a pencil and string, anchored at the center with a pin stuck into the working surface (see drawing opposite). You could also draw the circle by using a round object, such as a can, plate, pot cover, lampshade, etc.

To place the pattern on the circle, use auxiliary lines. Draw radii of the circle for guides. To find the center of circles for which you used objects as patterns, fold the circle in half and then half again. The center is where the lines (diameters) intersect.

These diameters are guide lines. Mark the fabric at the fold in the same way. The folds must be soft and made in the usual way. Check to make sure the fold is straight and that there is an equal distance between the diameters. Correct by cautiously making a new fold or a stylus mark or light pencil line. A long steel ruler is most helpful in textile printing work.

Dividing a circle into six pie-shaped pieces can easily be done by measuring. Measure the radius of the circle (half the diameter) on a piece of graph paper. Mark this distance six times on the circumference as shown in the drawing on page 86. Do not fold the material or paper more than three times, because the folds will become more and more inaccurate as you proceed.

CALCULATING DESIGNS FOR CIRCLES

It is a fixed rule that the prints must accentuate the circular shape, either by following the curvature or by following the radii toward the center.

Make test prints on paper or on fabric leftovers with the block you intend to use and place the prints along the arc of the circle. Mark them off with a pencil. A quarter segment of the circle you plan to use should be sufficient for a test of the design.

If you use triangular blocks, see that the base of the triangle fits into the circumference.

Mark the measurements of your design layout on the paper pattern you have cut out to use as a guide for printing.

PRINTING

Before you print on the material, make a final test print on paper. Print a complete section, that is, a quarter or a pie-segment, of the circle, to get the effect. The main rule is to start printing at the center and work outward, unless you are making just a border.

84

The center motif on a very large tablecloth, constructed on circles. We used only background blocks in greens and yellows.

How to draw large circles with a string and a pencil and a pin. Just roll the string around the pencil to make smaller diameters.

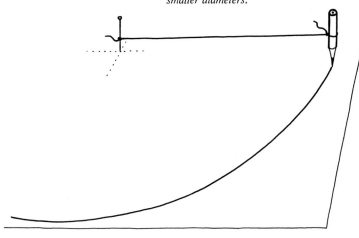

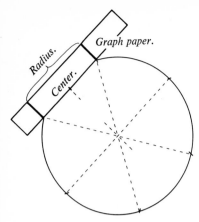

Radius.

Graph paper.

Center.

Dividing a circle with graph paper.

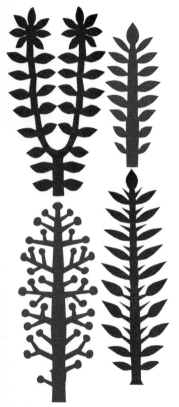

Stylized leaf ornamentation. Cut this out in a paper-cut and then transfer it to the linoleum block.

Place the circle—or the paper with the round hole—on the material while printing. Fasten it with tape or heavy weights. Print according to the marks and use the paper as a guide. If you think it is easier, just mark lightly on the material.

If you want to print several concentric circles within each other as in the photograph on page 85, you can cut out a paper pattern for each ring and mark the distance from circle to circle on diameters with fine pencil dots. Or you can use the pencil and string method to draw the concentric circles.

You can also use the circles directly as guides for the printing blocks by placing the prints against the edge of the paper. You can obtain triangles with a rounded base by printing over the cut-out circle, just as you used the paper mask (see page 57).

You can make a blank circle ring by covering the material with the paper circle pattern and printing over it with the block.

For background printing in a circle, use the piece of paper with the circle cut out as a mask. Place the first print out from the middle of the circle so the printing will be symmetrical.

Always save all paper patterns of this type for possible use later.

POSITIONING THE DESIGN

Many amateurs like to print around with triangular background blocks. This is fine, of course, but why not show a bit more imagination (see page 91)?

The drawing on the left shows the creation of a motif for a circle. The center circle may be open and without a pattern. Print the next circle with a leaf pattern following the radii. In the outer circle use a border motif that follows the extensions of the radii.

Place a cut-out paper circle in the middle when you print and mark off the measurements as radii along which you are going to print the leaves (if you don't want to mark lightly on the material).

When you print the outer border, draw auxiliary guide lines on the piece of brown paper left over after you cut your large circle.

The illustration at right top shows the edge of a large tablecloth printed with a similar leaf decoration on the radii using two colors or two shades of the same color.

The illustration with the circular center section marked shows how the same motif can be used in another way by changing the order of the prints, again using two colors.

The sketch above shows how the leaf patterns arranged in circles can be used as motifs on a long tablecloth.

You can cut out leaf motifs by folding a piece of paper and cutting, the way you do when you want to make cut-out human

86

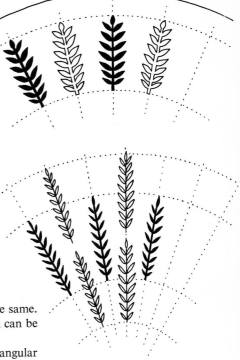

figures. This way you get both sides of the leaf exactly the same. The examples on page 86 were done this way. The pattern can be cut easily in linoleum.

Round motifs can be used on circular, square, and rectangular objects. They are very attractive on blouses, as described in the next project.

When you do a circular pattern that is continuous around the ring, you will find circular paper patterns useful, if you feel that guidelines drawn on the fabric may show on the finished print.

We intend to print the pattern above in two colors—dark and light. The light color is indicated by open leaves.

Overblouse—circular print

This pattern fits sizes 10–14, but the length, width, and sleeve length must be adjusted to the individual.

PATTERN LAYOUT

Fold washed and ironed material lengthwise and then fold once crosswise. Put the paper pattern on the fabric along the fold at the top and the side. Your paper pattern is one-quarter of the entire blouse or half of the front. By folding according to the directions and cutting through all four thicknesses of the fabric (DO NOT CUT

87

You can use round motifs in many other places than on round tablecloths. They are attractive on curtains, pillow covers, and rectangular tablecloths.

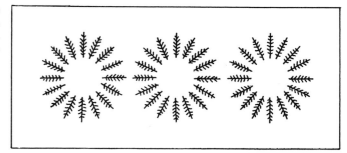

ALONG THE FOLD LINES) you will have the entire overblouse piece. Lay the pattern in place and cut. Remember to allow for seams.

Cut the cuff facings and the collar out of the four pieces of fabric left over from the space under the arm. Cut the collar on the bias so it will sit correctly when sewn. The collar must be $7\frac{7}{8}$ in. $\times$ $23\frac{5}{8}$ in. Piece it if necessary, as you would in joining any bias strips.

Sketch in the yoke design on the paper diagram. If it is going to be $4\frac{3}{4}$ in. wide, make pencil marks about 1 in. apart along the curve line $4\frac{3}{4}$ in. from the neck opening (see diagram). Connect these marks with a line to make a smooth curve. Now cut through the paper diagram along this line and use the upper part as a mask when you print the background.

If you are going to print a pattern on the yoke that requires masking, use the lower half of the paper pattern diagram for this.

Mark the border design area at the wrist.

PRINTING

Unfold the material that was cut double and stretch it out flat on the printing table. Turn the half you are going to print first toward you.

Cover up half of the yoke with the cut paper and keep it in place with heavy objects. Don't use pins as the paint may go through the holes when you move the pins.

Cover the borders on the sleeves the same way with paper.

As shown in the diagram on page 89, make the first background prints with the D block at the top of the middle of the overblouse. Print out along the fold of the sleeve in both directions.

When you make overblouses like this *start printing at the shoulder.* If you don't do that, the prints might become crooked, and then they won't fit when you print the first full row.

On the overblouse shown the background print is shifted half the width of the block to the side to make the brick pattern.

You can print the collar with the background color of the over-

Materials

Bleached or unbleached muslin about 55 in. wide by 60 in. long. This material usually shrinks about 10 per cent, so wash it before printing.

Blocks: Flat block D plus different patterned modular blocks.

Colors: About 7 oz. for the background print. Use paint leftovers for border motifs (really small amounts used).

88

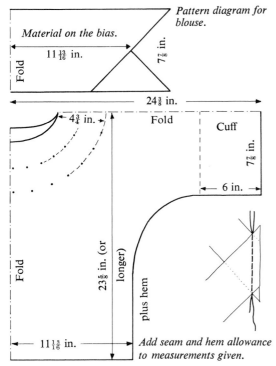

Pattern diagram for blouse.

Material on the bias.

11 13/16 in.

7 7/8 in.

Fold

24 3/8 in.

4 3/4 in.

Fold

Cuff

7 7/8 in.

6 in.

Fold

23 5/8 in. (or longer)

plus hem

11 13/16 in.

Add seam and hem allowance to measurements given.

Let your imagination go wild for this design. The pattern on this blouse was inspired by Mexican designs. Don't use overwhelming patterns and colors for small people.

blouse on the bottom half (this becomes the underside of the collar) suggested as "background color brown." On the half of the other long side print a patterned border up to the center fold. The last quarter of the collar, next to your neck, can be printed with one of the colors used for one of the pattern borders. We suggested turquoise. The same color should also be used for printing the underside, or lining, of the cuffs.

Use a background block for these parts of both the collar and cuffs.

DESIGN FOR THE YOKE

The most important part of the overblouse pattern is the rounded yoke and here is a good chance for you to use your imagination.

The drawings on page 90 show how a pattern can grow as it becomes larger and larger as you move away from the center. We used ovals cut in three different sizes. As they grow, they move further and further apart to give a harmonious impression.

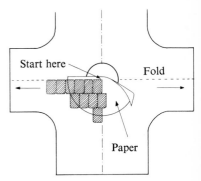

Start here

Fold

Paper

How to start to print.

89

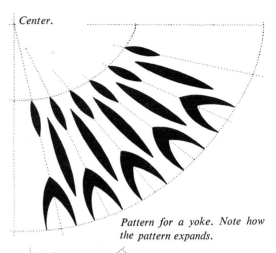

Pattern for a yoke. Note how the pattern expands.

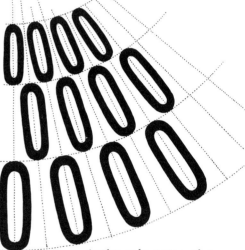

You can make a textile printed blouse for a little girl and a matching one for her doll. You must make the doll's blouse with an opening and a snap in the back because the head is too large to go through the neck opening. The background is printed with a cork block.

Another yoke pattern that grows, built of ovals that are larger in each ring.

| Turquoise. |
| Pattern border. ↕ |
| Background color: brown. |

Collar for the overblouse with suggestions for color selection.

90

Additional suggestions for yoke patterns. All are made from paper-cuts.

The other illustration opposite shows three related oval figures used in a similar manner. The suggestions on this page are made from folded cut paper (see page 92).

Triangular blocks with patterns

Patterned triangular blocks are good not only for making round prints but also for decorating overblouses. You can use them for borders and to fill in pattern areas, too. Build up the pattern according to the nature of the triangle, that is, follow the base line and

91

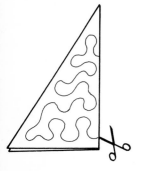

hypothetical middle axis, which is shown as a dotted line on the diagram. If you wish, make the pattern in a Christmas-tree shape.

The easiest way to make triangular patterns is to cut them. Cut out a piece of black paper the size of the triangular block. Fold it along the middle axis and cut into the paper from the fold or from the sides. This way you get a symmetrical pattern. Glue the cut-out patterns on white paper and save them for future use.

The drawings suggest different designs. Some of them can also be used for repeat printing to give a uniform design over a whole surface. You can use triangular blocks for centre borders with background prints on both sides.

If the paper is not too thin, use it as a template or stencil to transfer the pattern to the block. If the cuts are small, transfer the entire pattern to transparent paper so you can transfer it to the block with carbon paper, as described earlier.

Pattern overprinting and two-color blocks

If you print one color on top of another color, you will have a third color as a result. Earlier in the book we showed examples of this. The third color is a result of an *optical* mixing rather than a

The pattern must fit the triangular form and must be done so that it follows the base line and hypothetical center axis (above). Cut the pattern with scissors after you fold the paper on the center axis of the triangle. Make the cut from the fold, the outer edge, or from both sides of the drawing.

physical mixing. Physical mixing would be a direct mixing of the color substances or ingredients.

The optical mixing is an effect that can be exploited in many different ways. You can, of course, make overprints on the background prints, but you can also print with two pattern blocks, one on top of the other, to bring forth a completely new pattern.

There is, however, a limit to how many times you can overprint. The paint layer can easily become too thick and the material uncomfortably stiff at the printed areas. This stiffness, which may also result from inferior paint quality, must definitely be avoided. You should not be able to feel the paint on the material at all. Another problem is that with excessive overprinting the colors become muddy and unclear. Note that on our printed tablecloth shown on page 74 we did not print more than twice over the same area, *despite* the many printings.

Through this overprint technique, as we have seen, you can also make a darker shade if you print with the same color twice.

You can cut patterns in various colors of tissue paper. When these cut patterns are placed over one another you can see the color effect of overprinting.

Drawing 1. These four leaves have been cut in one block.

Drawing 2. Here we printed with the same block (1) twice but without overprinting. We just turned the block so that the four leaves became one flower with eight petals.

Drawing 3. The same design, here cut a bit smaller, was combined with another flower-shaped design. This can be cut on the same block or it can be made by combining two blocks.

Drawing 4. The previous figure was overprinted on top of itself with the block turned. A more complicated flower was the result, and at the same time we got a negative picture in the middle.

Drawing 5. In this case the four leaves from drawing 1 are paired with the flower from drawing 3. We used two colors.

Drawing 6. This last example shows the block from the third drawing overprinted with the four-leaf (or *quatrefoil* as this figure is called) block turned.

You can make thousands of similar examples by overprinting patterns where color plays a part. Experimentation with such figures will give you experience in combining patterns. This exercise will repay you many times over in working with textile printing.

POSSIBILITIES:

When you print with two colors you have the following possibilities:

93

5

6

1. Background completely or partly covered by another background print.
2. Background print overprinted with patterned block with a different color.
3. Print twice with the same patterned or background block, one print on top of the other, turning the block between printings.
4. Change the colors, but without overprinting.
5. Shifted printing.
6. Coloration printing or coloring in parts of the pattern, such as leaves that were printed as an outline only, overprinted, or filled in, with green color.

Block for two-color print. Use a saw to separate the rider and the horse, so you can print each with its own color. You can also assemble them to print the entire block with one color. In a two-color print it would be tempting to brush on the color and save a block, but this procedure should be avoided since the print will not only lose the character of a textile print, but it will also be ugly.

94

INDEX